50 Things They <u>D</u>

Dedicated to Crystal, the love of my life. Thank you, Haylee and Garrett for showing me what love is.

Be Great Now!

Ti

Foreword

These 50 lessons are wonderful to integrate into your life and was a reminder for me to do better on a few of them. Tim is so consistent at implementing them and that is why he stands out as the best in the industry.

You don't need great sales skills starting off, but if you make a habit of implementing these lessons, I know you will have people wanting to buy from you, along with everyone enjoying being around you.

I wish I had read a book like this when I started out as a young sales guy. Take the lessons and run with them. Make them your own. I'm confident you'll set yourself apart and be exceptional. I've seen it first-hand.

Tim is a special person and whenever I get to see him it's a great feeling. He created that great feeling and you can, too.

Lance Dean

Co-Founder, 2gig Technologies,

Founder of Guru Alert.

Introduction

Thank you for picking up my book. I decided to write it in an effort to help anyone coming from nothing who desires freedom and wealth. In my life, I value both financial and personal freedom. It took years to create a wonderful environment, and I've made my share of mistakes and good moves along the way. If you aren't where you want to be in life, I think you will find many of the following 50 points helpful. Whether you are 10 years of age or 110, I promise you there will be value in the chapters to follow!

I'm a multiple business owner, but I'm proud to say that I've earned my living in sales, and have built my modest wealth in real estate. There will be a lot of sales and real estate-related material in this book.

The three businesses that I own are:

A Security Representation Business, where we sell security equipment to installing alarm companies called Personal Alarm Representation (PAR).

Secondly, a Promotional Products business where we can put any business logo on millions of different items like pens and shirts, called GoLogo.

Finally, Real Estate business where I own rental properties, I buy rental properties with the intention to hold them forever and create wealth with appreciation and debt reduction. Let me speak to each of these businesses.

The Security Representation Business was started in 1998 mainly out of the desire to no longer reside permanently in corporate America. Secondly, because I'm an entrepreneur at heart and would rather call on independent businessmen than corporate customers; I just relate better to them. In this business we represent 30 product lines in a 4 state region. Companies use representation firms like ours instead of employees and sometimes in conjunction with employees. The benefit for the companies using reps like us is that they get territorial sales coverage for a fixed percentage of sales like 5-10%. For the manufacturer this is predictable and normally less expensive than an employee with benefits and expenses. The manufacturers also benefit from our 25-plus-year relationships with the customers. Day in and day out in this business, our company PAR Products (www.parproducts.com) calls on installing security companies, think ADT and the thousands of smaller competitors and wholesale distributors where the alarm companies get their parts, like ADI and Tri-Ed. Our goal is for companies that install alarm systems in businesses and homes to use our products instead of our competitors. Ernie, Kyle, Craig, and Crystal do a tremendous job in this fun business. I was lucky to get into this recession-proof business at a young age. I always say, "in good times people are building, thus using new security gear, and in bad times, unfortunately, the crime rates increase and people are breaking in and there is more need for security." The security business usually does well regardless of what's going on in the economy. As a young person trying to find a recession-proof business, I got lucky!

    The Promotional Products Company, GOLOGO (www.mygologo.com) was spun out of an idea I had in 1994 of a Koozie (beer can insulator) that could fit in a golf cart, The Cart Cooly. Basically, the shape of every fast food to-go cup, but in a Koozie form before that shape was everywhere. After selling the Cart Cooly exclusively with corporate logos, people would ask, "Could you do golf balls, shirts, etc.?" That led us to offer every product under the sun with a logo on it. Over time, the Cart Cooly became too expensive to produce, but thankfully for that little invention, a lot of good came for a lot of people! A lot of people didn't have to drink warm beer.

The best thing that came out of it was being able to afford to move my parents from cold Chicago to Dallas. GoLogo is now a full-service promotional products company. We can put your logo on virtually anything! This business does over $2.5M in sales, and the average order size is $400. As you can imagine, a lot of attention to detail comes with this fun business. Bobbi Jo, Bryon, Ashlee, Courtney, and on occasion Will, are awesome, and I'm lucky to get to work with such a great group!

Real Estate Business—I have always had a passion for Real Estate as far back as my desire to own my own home before I was 20 years old! I did it at 19 and 10 months. I currently have 158 people paying me rent each month, (I have adjusted this number up four times since the start of writing the book. I just can't stop buying great investments.) My properties range from great homes in Southlake, Texas, an affluent area outside of Dallas, to small apartment buildings in semi-rural Kentucky (www.kyapt.com). My philosophy on real estate rentals is that if the property is pretty it can be negative cash flow for a few years (rents don't cover the cost of mortgage). If it's ugly, it has to make money on Day One. The "pretty" high-end properties make money long term because they typically appreciate rapidly over time, rents increase, and the properties go up in value. The "ugly" ones appreciate rather slowly, so they need to make money immediately. We will talk a fair amount about leverage in the book and real estate, when you only put 10-20% down and you get to keep 100% of the gains. This is a great way to leverage your money and put it to work. Very few new fortunes have been made without leverage. If you understand both the upside and downside of leverage, you will understand that it is an extremely good tool for creating wealth faster than some other methods.

At the end of the day, I proudly consider myself a Salesman. Sales is a great judge of what you are doing right or wrong. Sales reward you each day, month, and year. Sales will let you know real quickly what you are doing well and what you need to improve on. I don't believe that there are that many, "Born Salesmen". I surely wasn't one. It's a skill set that takes time to learn, like every other trade. The challenge with sales is the tremendous amount of rejection and the people who "try sales" and fail, then rule out sales for life. I think that's crazy. Were you good at riding a bike, driving a car, or hitting a golf ball the first time you did that? Why should you be good at sales right out of the gate? The difference is other things you fail at don't give you as much personal rejection as sales. As a young guy, I got super lucky to be hired by two tremendous salesmen. I am lucky that Lance Dean saw that I was a hard-working bartender, and might do well in sales. He was kind enough to hire me into the security business. Both Lance and I reported to Ben Cornett, who might be the best salesman I have ever known and probably the best relationship guy there is. Lance grew to be every bit as good as Ben; some say better. I'm so thankful to have met these two men. I love them both so much that I can't pick a favorite between the two of them. There is no way I could have achieved my modest level of success without meeting these two people at the young age I did. Ben is 20 years my senior and Lance is 3 years older. Meeting and learning from great mentors at a young age changes your success trajectory over a lifetime.

We were all working for a company that made a sensor, which detected glass breaking (Blue Grass Electronics, based in Lagrange, KY). This Glass Break Sensor would then be wired back to an alarm control panel. Back in 1988, it was a nice company full of young, energetic salesmen doing $6 million worth of sales annually. But the lessons learned were priceless! I suggest that as a young person the people you can learn from mean more than the job you are currently working at. It always amazes me that someone will try to get into the best college, but once they have graduated they will take the highest-paying job, regardless of whether they will have great mentors to learn from. Students will take on $100K in college debt but take the wrong job without mentors to learn from because it pays $5K a year more? Craziness! In my mind, it's just like in the dictionary: mentors come before money.

There are millions of people more successful than I. Why is it that I feel like I have the right to write a book? Why would you take your valuable time to read it? The driving forces are:

First, I have read more than 700 books and very few give you basic blocking and tackling common sense on how to start from nothing and achieve some level of success. I have found that most books focused on just one concept for 300 pages. This book is more diverse. According to Tim Ferriss, author of 4 Hour Work Week, fewer than 5% of the 195,000 books published each year sell more than 5,000 copies. I'm not writing this book with the vision of grandeur; I'm writing this to help others. All proceeds will go to the community storehouse food pantry in Keller, Texas. At the end of my book, I have a list of my favorite books. Robert Kiyosaki, author of the Rich Dad Poor Dad series, is right up there with everything the late great Zig Ziglar wrote. I love everything Grant Cardone has written, especially a book called 10X, while the tough no-nonsense style of Jeffrey Gitomer is the right potion if you are having a pity party. Maybe the original positive salesperson writer is the late Napoleon Hill. His words helped mold my thinking as a young man.

If you get bored easily, I think my book will keep your attention. If a particular chapter isn't for you, skip it and go to the next! In school, if you get 9 out 10 questions right you get an A, so if something isn't clicking with you go to next chapter. I would have loved to read this book at age 20. This book will cover everything from the importance of "thank you" notes to leveraging money, to having a generous aura about you. Secondly, people say that I'm self-made because I didn't have family money or married into money. I truly feel no one is self-made. We are all a product of the opportunities around ourselves, and choosing to learn lessons, and embracing the knowledge from people that know more than you. I look for sharper people than me and learn from them. School is never out for me. When forced to be around negative and unmotivated people, I observed and noted their behavior so I continue to learn what not to do.

There are many books that are from a more-polished perspective, but if you are interested in hearing REAL life lessons from a kid who collected aluminum cans and bottles (back in the day you could turn them in for a nickel or dime) for money, delivered papers, washed dishes, worked in a factory, worked in restaurants, was a lousy salesman and grew to become a fun loving, generous multi-millionaire, this is the book for you. It's great to know you don't have to score perfect on your SAT or be extremely gifted to achieve a very happy, financially free and prosperous life.

People often ask me how I got started. What were my influences? I hear often that I look at things differently, and where did you get that perspective? Most people don't achieve financial and personal freedom, so following the mass thinking all but guarantees you won't have a different and favorable outcome. There will be a lot of financial information in this book, and if you don't know me you might think it's all about money and/or material things. People who really know me would say that I am generous with my time and money. The only thing money does for me, is that it gives me freedom of choices, and I strongly desire the freedom to do the right thing every day. Money allows more free choices. This morning, I passed a group of 10 servicemen in the airport. I reached into my pocket pulled out a $100 bill, thanked them for their service, and told them breakfast was on me. I'm thrilled I could do that; $100 isn't going to change my life, but hopefully my gesture made their day! I am humble and extremely blessed to have a great positive attitude and I managed to create a life that I truly enjoy each and every day. So here you go... everything opened up. Here are the 50 things that I've learned with my 50 years on the planet. Enjoy!

Chapters

1

Be Great Now

My parents Charlie and Marge Shiner at Easter 2010.

Be great at whatever job you currently have at this time, and if at all possible have a portion of your compensation earned by commission or tips. Some of my first jobs were: paperboy, busboy, waiter, bartender.

One of my favorite lines I ask, "Do you think Michael Jordan started practicing free throws when he got to the NBA or do you think because he practiced free throws when he was just Mike Jordan, he got to the NBA?!" I think if you start settling at a very young age, you stunt your potential successes by not kicking it into gear at a young age. You lower your trajectory of success. I always viewed working hard as a fun game.

When I was 14 years old, I was working as a busboy. I would try to carry more dishes to the back than the other busboys. I would race to get bread and water to a table just as soon as the customers were seated. It was a race and a game in my mind. I would call my shot with waitresses to let them know I was going to bust my butt for them. I would go up to the waitresses and let them know at the start of the night that they were going to turn more tables (the quicker you clean up a table and get it seated again) and thus make more money with me in their section. Call your shot, then deliver! I would go above and beyond filling drinks, cleaning tables, getting bread, checking on overall satisfaction, really the waitress' job.

I did this consciously for three reasons. One was to be the best busboy at Cheddar's Restaurant and TGI Fridays. Two, to make more tips, the waitress tip out the busboys at the end of the night, so the more money they made, the more they would tip out to me. And three, I was training myself for my next job, being a waiter. Like a mini-Jordan I was shooting free throws before my next step, becoming a waiter. Once I became a waiter, I was helping out the bar staff, and learning drinks to make sure if there was ever an opening behind the bar, I would be the logical choice.

I was a bartender at 19 years old; every other bartender was much older than me. In fact, the liquor law was changed to 21, but fortunately they grandfather in the younger folks that were already working in the industry. So I wasn't old enough to drink anymore but I could serve it. You have to be a go-getter from the word "go" and never with the mindset, "I'm going to turn it on when I'm 'blank' or when I'm 'some age'.

Turn it on right now and never turn it off! You have 76% of your week to do whatever you want!! If you work a 40-hour work week, and there are 168 hours in a week that means 24% of your time spent working so bust your ass!! If you want to be great work 50 hours (70% time off) or even a harder worker at 60 hours a week and have 64% of your time to yourself! No excuses for not being great at what you do! You would have to work 84 hours a week to be at 50% of your time, and that would be working double what most people do and that still leaves you half of your week to yourself. Now I know you have to sleep, but this is to show how little time you actually have to work. If you have to be at work, work as hard as you can.

When I was a waiter at Cheddar's restaurants in both Arlington and Bedford, Texas, I would try to trade into a better section to work in an effort to maximize my opportunity to make money while at work. In addition, when the night got slower with fewer customers, managers would start cutting staff. I would always stay later to work more. My thought was if I took the time, effort, and energy to get dressed and drive to work I was going to work as hard as I could and as long as I could to, quite frankly, make as much money as I could while I was there. When you are young and have very few skills, the only skill you can control is your work ethic.

The lesson I learned by being a busboy, waiter, and bartender was the better you took care of people the more money you made. That experience trained me to be a future salesman. You also received the satisfaction that you made a difference and made the customer's night better.

I strongly suggest young people work at a job where you can make gratuity (tips). It's the perfect primer in life to teach you how to hustle, sell, and take care of others. In life, the more value

14

you bring to others, the more money, and satisfaction you receive in return. I remember the first tip in my life. It was a quarter, and I received it about 36-37 years ago. I was on my early morning paper route, and it was a rainy cold Chicago Morning. I didn't want to be in the weather for sure; no one would want to walk to the end of the driveway to get their paper, even though it was safely wrapped in a protective plastic bag. I took the extra time to ride my bike up to each and every porch to place the paper on the safe, dry porches.

A kind man recognized my extra effort and reached into his pocket, gave me a quarter and said, "Thank you. I appreciate your extra effort". That's it. then and there I was hooked on giving extra effort and hooked, on a lifetime of pointing out, complimenting, and rewarding extra effort! We all know people who do the bare minimum in life, right? Think about those people. What does life give back to them? The bare minimum right back at them! Give more get more, give very little, get very little. Our lives aren't a dress rehearsal; this is it on earth (yes, I believe there is a heaven) so live your life on earth in a way that you can achieve and enjoy your dreams. Go above and beyond, so you can receive above and beyond joys in life. If you have done absolutely nothing above average, you would be crazy to expect anything above average to come back your way! When it comes to effort life is fair. It gives you back what you put into it. Start today whether you're 10, 18, 33, 42, 50 or 82 to be the best at whatever you do!

2

The Joy of Generosity

Team Audrey! Her second Dallas marathon with her
supporters pushing her. GoLogo donated shirts.

Be extremely generous, not just generous, but over the top, memorable generous. It doesn't have to be monetary. Be generous with help, or time, or a compliment. Make someone's day and make a difference! One of my definitions of faith is being generous before you have it made in life. Shows that you know and believe without a doubt you will get to that place you are dreaming of. I was married from 21-31 years old, and this was a re-occurring fight. My ex-wife would say, "Why are we giving away money before we are very well off?" All I knew was the more generous I was, the better I felt and the more successful I became. Call it Karma, the law of attraction, or the aura of being a giver. Whatever it is, it has worked in my life! I've never understood why you would hoard money and then very late in life or after you're dead, then become generous? You missed the fun, hopefully an 80- to 90-year generous ride! I rarely turn down a meeting with a friend in need or someone who is looking to chat. I consider that being generous with your most precious evaporating commodity—time.

There are so many things you can be generous with:

A. Airline miles. Crystal, my wife, is a Southwest Airlines flight attendant and every bit of one, just a ball of sunshine. She was flying with a great lady whose son was a backup QB for an NFL team and was going to get his first NFL start because his team had already clinched a playoff spot and the team was going to put their backups on the field for that game. The challenge was SWA didn't fly to Charlotte, NC, and both she and her husband had to be back to Dallas for work on Monday morning after the Sunday game. I had an abundant amount of American Airline miles, so we gave them two AA confirmed tickets to see their son play. As fate would have it, that team later went on to win their first Super Bowl that year and the signed football sent as a thank you still sits in our son Garrett's room.

B. Match Charity dollars. As a young salesman my boss Ben created a program one year that he would match with company dollars with any dollars the employees donated for needy families at Christmas. I believe I gave $500, which was a tremendous amount for me at the time, but the thought that my $500 would turn into $1,000 was just too exciting not to max out. Ben was shocked at the amount, but I felt so good knowing my money was being matched and would do exponential good. Once you look, there are many opportunities to donate money where matching funds are available. A few times a year, my local food bank has a donor who matches funds received during a small window of time. Many employers match charitable funds donated. You can always be the one who matches funds donated by others.

C. Donate products. We are fortunate to have a promotional products business (we put logos on things like shirts and hats etc.) I love donating gear to great causes or big birthdays like turning 40 or 50, cancer awareness walks, kids' sports teams, weddings, or supporting a cause important to a good friend. The amount of appreciation you get back is amazing! For whatever reason folks don't know where to get small amounts of custom printing koozies, T-shirts, etc. It's fun to help with causes that are important to others—really unforgettable to the recipient. Tommy Burdette, the salesman working for a distributor in the security business in Houston was coming to Dallas because his wife was doing a truly amazing event. This is a story about three great girlfriends. Unfortunately, Audrey, one of the girls got into a horrific car accident while going to Kinko's to make copies of a college paper. Audrey was fighting an 18-month battle and was in a wheelchair. Her two friends would be running the marathon, pushing dedicating themselves to 13.1 miles pushing Audrey in the wheelchair. So touched by this, we not only did custom Under Armour shirts for the three gals, but also for their spouses, a dozen friends, and family members and we also donated the use of our condo in Dallas for them to stay and enjoy themselves. It cost us very little to help make an awesome memory!

D. One of my best friends is Jim Zadeh. His father was an extremely generous man that emigrated from Iran to America with less than $500 in his pocket. He became a doctor and did well, but his legacy that I learned more about at his funeral was how many people he had helped financially to come to America. When you look at how generous he was, how many lives he touched and how those people then had kids, it is truly amazing what one gesture can turn into. When Dr. Zadeh passed away, his family started a scholarship fund with the goal of helping one immigrant per year with a $10K endowment. Seeing the legacy of a 92-year-old life motivated me to help a person come to America. Dr. Zadeh lived a generous life; he would never take money from me when he fixed an ailment. He would just say, "Do something nice for someone in need" and "thanks for being a good friend to my son." What an amazing legacy and a tremendous goal to be as giving as him.

The down side of being generous is you being a sucker and people taking advantage of you. I promise you I am taken advantage of all the time and at times it becomes challenging. It's just a byproduct of being generous, just like strikeouts are a byproduct of hitting home runs. Focus on the home runs of generosity. I often say that there are Givers and Takers in the world. The challenge is both Givers and Takers are seeking the same person; the Giver. At times, two Givers can't find each other because they each are being occupied by a Taker. I am blessed to be married to the sweetest Giver I have ever met. Whatever challenges I've incurred, the joy of generosity has been well worth it.

3

Thank Your Way to the Top

Writing thank you notes with my cat Bianca 1991. Follow up changed my life!

Write thank you notes, not text or emails. Those are average and ordinary. You can still do those, but thank you notes are gold nuggets and texts are tin. In my mind, a written note is 50Xs more powerful. It shows that you really care. It creates a deeper friendship and bond. I'm not saying don't text and email; do those things too! Your follow up isn't done until you send a thank you note through the good ole' U.S. mail. I'm not sure everyone does this, but I wait till the end of going through my mail to open anything that looks remotely good, like a thank you note. It's my treat after dealing with mortgage statements, bills, etc. If you ask anyone who was the last person to send them a hand written thank you note, not only can they recall who, but they can tell you when, and what it was for. Ask them who texted or emailed them last Wednesday around noon and they have no clue. It's that valuable! The value of being a thank-you note writer is only going up in years to come, so this one great habit will be more valuable in years to come because technology is just too easy.

I first tried writing thank you notes in 1988 after attending a Tom Hopkins seminar in Kansas City. I was a young struggling salesperson. I took my customer, Paul Straten—who was working for a great security company called National Guardian—to the seminar with me because I felt guilty that I was out of town on business with expenses of the hotel, rent car, etc., and wasn't seeing four to five customers that day. Tom Hopkins is a motivational speaker who made his money in California real estate as a sales person. Quite frankly, he really came off as cheesy. With every meeting, seminar or event I focus on trying to learn just one thing from the other person that they do better than me and try to incorporate that into my personality. Seriously I do this every day. By doing this, even in a bad situation, you can find something positive, even if it's learning what NOT to do.

Back to Mr. Hopkins, he did two memorable things that day, one he asked a question with a long drawn out approach that was demeaning to the person being asked the question (kind of I'm smarter than you attitude) so I learned not to do that! But the multi-million dollar gem he gave me was Thank You notes! This $99 dollar seminar has paid out millions. Talk about a return on investment! It's said that it takes 21 days to turn a behavior into a habit. I decided that I would try Tom Hopkins' thank you notes suggestion for 30 days before I made a decision to quit or keep it for life. To hold myself to this goal, I kept a journal of who I sent thank you notes to, for the benefit of seeing if those individuals were more receptive to me in the future and to keep score because when you are writing thank you notes it's a lot of lonely work. In addition, I wasn't sure it was going to work and I wanted to journal my experiment.

I went crazy with these things. If someone basically kicked me out of their office a note went like this, "thank you for giving me a moment of your time today, I love successful, busy people like yourself, looking forward to the opportunity to sit down and help you become even more successful". For real, you kick me out of your office; you get a thank you note! So guess what happened? I still was an unskilled, but a more likable young salesman. However, now I had adopted the professional skill of "follow up" by writing thank you notes. As you would probably expect, folks were more willing to see me, buy from me, and help me because I was slowly becoming a young professional salesman. An added byproduct bonus was that I started to remember people's names much better because I was writing them a note and writing their address on an envelope.

Tons of people have a hard time remembering other people's names; this is a great byproduct of written thank you notes. You are never too old or too good of friends with someone to write them a thank you note.

I'm going to rat out a buddy, but keep his name out of it. I really like this guy, but it's too good of an example to not share. I've had a 10-year relationship with my buddy that sold me my 1st Lamborghini, from Lamborghini of Dallas. I've helped him with home security stuff for free. He left Lambo of Dallas for a few years (people don't buy Lambos in a recession), and I tried to get him a job. He literally said I was the only person who tried to help him get a job. He's invited me to car rallies, sneak previews of the baddest new Lambos, etc. Right before Thanksgiving 2013 I had a small financial windfall (sold a lot in a prestigious neighborhood) and decided to buy a used 2003 Ferrari 360 convertible, with only 3,000 miles. I grabbed my stepson Garrett, drove to the dealership, and haggled a little with my salesman buddy. We agreed on a price, and I drove away in the Ferrari and he got a $100K sale! It took maybe two hours, with an hour of that Garrett and I having lunch, trying to get a lower price. Sure enough, an envelope from Lambo of Dallas showed up a week later, and I knew my buddy had done the right thing: he sold a Ferrari and I was getting a thank you card, right? Wrong! It was a generic Christmas card from the car dealership. How in the world as a professional sales person who has sold me more than $250K worth of cars (Update, now over $550K), not take four minutes to write a thank you card?

You know what happens when you buy a Ferrari? Everyone, and I mean everyone, asks you where you got it. You could walk around town with a Unicorn (I promised my buddy Ainslie Fukuda from Wave Electronics I would work a Unicorn into the book) and folks wouldn't ask you where you got it as much as a Ferrari. So my point is, if everyone asking you where you got it would my buddy like to hear me say my good friend "blank" at Lambo of Dallas?! He probably sold four to six cars all month. So let's say its six cars times four minutes. You don't have 24 minutes out of a 160 hours that month to thank guys for buying cars between $100K and half a million dollars? I still buy cars from my buddy because he has a ton of great qualities, but I secretly wonder how much better my friend could be doing with thank you notes.

I'm here to tell you that I will be on my deathbed and I still will be sending thank you notes. If you are a professional you have to follow up with written thank you notes. My old boss, Ben Cornett, (get used to hearing his name, because he is the MAN and he is in the book a lot!) always said only thank the customers you want to keep. Well, customers are too hard to get to begin with, so I'm going to be the salesman who will ALWAYS thanks them forever! I've written over 20,000 thank you notes so far and hope to write another 20,000! I might not always be the best salesman at any given time, but I will always be the best follow up guy!

Update- Right before this book went to print I got a thank you note from my car guy! Threw it out in the universe and things happened!

4

Remembering Your Mentors

Lance Dean and I holding Ben Cornett.

Continually thank and praise your mentors in life, throughout your life. Give credit where credit is due. This helps you remember that you have had a fortunate and blessed life. Your mentors invested in you like a great stock, the dividend they should get back is your long-lasting appreciation and thankfulness toward them.

My two biggest mentors are Lance Dean and Ben Cornett. I thank these guys often, but here we go again. My life wouldn't be as wonderful as I feel it is without all the knowledge and lessons they both have taught me over the last 28 years. Thank you Lance and Ben for taking a chance on a young hard-working kid who didn't know a thing about sales. I naively thought that to be good in sales you had to talk a lot. There's an old saying that goes something like, "You have two ears, and one mouth as a salesman; use them in that correct ratio, listen twice as much as you talk". Funny story; and I still do it to this day. Lance taught me to listen by literally putting my hand over my mouth when visiting with a customer. I was so very excited about what I was selling that I couldn't wait to talk about it! Thank you Lance and Ben! Find mentors; when you see someone doing what you want to do, make them your friend. Ask about what they learned and how they learned it.

I chuckle over this childhood story. My dad, Charlie Shiner, was a general manager of a facility that made bottle caps. The company was called Kerr Glass (same Kerr as the home canning jars). This was around 1975, and the owner of a steel company that sold Kerr their steel took our family to Brunch in a very affluent Chicago north shore country club. We were living in a home that was less than a 2100 square feet and normal food at best, so brunch for a 10-year-old kid was an amazing event! Always a car nut, I walked around the country club admiring Mercedes, Cadillacs, Porsches, etc.

Halfway through this amazing event, I couldn't take it anymore! I looked the very well dressed successful man in the eye and asked, "Sir, how did you make your money?" I immediately got kicked underneath the table by my parents, I could tell the man wasn't offended and quickly answered, "You need to own something." I had no clue what that meant, but he had some of the answers to the questions I had in life. I would love to be mentored by him at a young age of 10, but I had zero value to give him in return. Moving forward, if I was a young kid again and saw someone with knowledge I wanted to gain, I would wash their car, work for free, anything! They have some of the answers I'm searching for – I have to bring value for them to allow me to linger around.

Mark Cuban was under some criticism recently for saying that interns shouldn't expect to be paid because what the intern was receiving was knowledge and that was far greater than money. Critics were saying Mark is rich so why not pay the interns? People were complaining that the rich guy was getting richer by using the interns. I totally disagree and I 100% agree with Mr. Cuban. What you can learn from him is priceless. Truth be told when I was a young salesperson learning from Ben and Lance, I should have been paying them! By far, I got more knowledge from them that has made me millions than they got from me selling some widgets for them. Seek and find mentors, but realize they are doing you a favor—so take out their garbage, mow their lawn, whatever—because the advice you are learning applied over a lifetime is truly priceless!

It was and is in my case. My new friend Jeff Costello (www.corebrands.com) has college age daughters, and he says that your 20s are for learning and networking. You probably aren't going to make that much difference monetarily between two jobs so focus on mentors, learning and meeting as many people as you can. Jeff and I are saying the same thing – focus on what you can learn, the dollars will follow.

5

Encourage the Next Generation

Jordan Okeefe's 16th Birthday

Be generous and thoughtful to your friends' children. Most people would rather that you do for their kids than for them. It's a tremendous compliment to be good to your friends' children. It also helps a child to see another adult think well of them. If you think back to your childhood, you can remember that great relative or family friend who was a positive example and influence. My uncle Ronnie was a huge influence. He owned an independent insurance agency and was very generous. There aren't that many of them out there; you need to be one of them!

When I receive high school graduation announcements, I normally respond with $100 and an opportunity for the would-be graduate to earn another $100 by writing me back with a list of written goals. It's a win-win-win. My friend's child gets $100 if they do nothing more. The second win kicks in when they actually take the time to write their goals (surprisingly 80-90% actually write back with written goals) and the third win hits when I send a kind note of encouragement with the additional $100.

There are a lot of opportunities between birth and graduation to be helpful and thoughtful to your friends' children. One of my favorite and oldest lines I represent in the Security business is a universal Key FOB that arms and disarms security panels, called Street Smart now owned by Honeywell. My boss for that line is Mark O'Keefe who lives in the second best city in America, San Diego, but he's from the best city, Dallas. His wife Lynn called me a month before some monumental birthdays. Their son Jordan was turning 16 over this spring break and Mark would be 45 that same week. She told me she was thinking about surprising them and flying them to Dallas for a few days! I made a deal with her: you get them to Dallas and I would have the rest covered. So they came, and, in one day, Jordan got to drive a Ferrari, drive a Lambo, sit courtside at a Mavs basketball game (which they won in the final seconds to clinch a playoff spot) and saw himself on Sports Center with his dad. Talk about a day!

Mark is a dialed-in great father. There is simply nothing I could do for Mark that would have measured up to what we could do for his son. It's not money. It's the freedom that money allows you the opportunity to do great things for great people. Talk about a real life "Ferris Bueller's Day Off"! Jordan did his part. I got a Top 10 best thank you card I have ever received a week later from him. Thank you Jordan for that first-class follow up! What made his thank you card so great was his sincerity and genuine appreciation.

6

R-E-S-P-E-C-T

Chicago Bears great, Jim McMahon and I. In 1985, Jim gave
Pete Rozelle more notoriety by wearing a headband with
"Rozelle" written on it.

Sounds simple, but so many people fail at it. Treat everyone with respect; maybe if you grew up doing as many low level jobs as I did, it would be easier to relate. I had the good fortune to collect aluminum cans for recycling money, got lucky to gather up soda bottles for deposit money (if you aren't sure what that is, ask someone with gray hair to explain it to you), shoveled driveways clear of snow in winters, mowed lawns in summers, and finally was a year around paper boy. I did all of this until I was old enough to lie about my age to be a busboy and bus tables at age 14 at an upscale Italian restaurant.

My busboy career lasted from 14-17 at various restaurants. Working these jobs taught me how to answer others with, "yes, sir and yes, ma'am," answering with respect to everyone. Always being a can-do guy, I would do virtually anything asked of me: cook, run food to tables, wash dishes. My managers at various restaurants knew if they called me the answer was "yes." I would do any job that somebody didn't show up for. I would usually be fair on dollars per hour, but knowing they could give away vouchers for free dinner for two people (comped meals) that was always part of my negotiation. As a young guy, that dinner for two was a great date night. When most guys my age were taking their dates to McDonalds or Burger King, my date and I were going to TGI Fridays, when Fridays was the place!

Back to the point, folks doing lower level or lower-paying jobs need your kind words more than most people. It's free and easy to give respect, a smile and a kind word. Who knows what their hopes and dreams are and maybe your kind words can put a pep in their step. Simply telling someone they are great at what they do is huge to the person. Looking or asking someone their name, remembering it and calling them by it is so powerful! You are never too rich or too poor to give away kind words. Nothing drives me crazier than someone looking down or acting above another person.

I was visiting my friend Chris who manages the car wash I go to, and he made a comment one day about how nice I always am. I said to him why wouldn't I be nice? He said so many people were rude and looked and spoke down to him. That's nuts. Why act above anyone, especially a nice guy like Chris. If you are blessed and lucky enough to be living a good or fortunate life, be thankful! Give respect to everyone around you; you don't know what challenges they might be going through. I have always thought that the receptionist or secretary has way more power than most people think.

I recently read the biography of the late, great Pete Rozelle, former commissioner of the NFL in the early years 1960-1989. What a great man and apparently a world-class listener and problem-solver. When he was planning to retire, Mr. Rozelle was in the process of looking for his replacement. It got down to two candidates, and one of them was constantly disrespectful to Mr. Rozelle's right-hand person, Thelma. Mr. Rozelle was known as a selfless person and was concerned that if this candidate wasn't pleasant to everyone, then maybe he wasn't the correct choice to represent the highest office in the NFL. You never know what information gets back to people. The candidate that chose not to be respectful to everyone never became commissioner of the NFL. Mr. Rozelle helped the NFL owners choose the more respectful Paul Tagliabue. Partly because of his respect for others, he held that office from 1989-2006. I have seen many times people not get opportunities because a comment here or information surfacing that was negative from their past tilts the opportunity to someone else.

Since very few people have sit down with a prolific active serial killer and tried to sell them on their point of view, I felt compelled to tell my story in this chapter.

In 1988, I was a young salesman working for Blue Grass Electronics selling Glass Break Detectors. We were fortunate as a company to have the opportunity to sell glass break detectors to ADT, the largest security company. Thanks to both Lance Dean and Ben Cornett, we were on the approved to sell list at ADT. Living in Chicago, I was responsible for a large Midwest territory that included both Kansas City and Wichita, Kansas. I was calling on the Kansas City office where I had some friendships. I asked for advice on how to get the Wichita office on board? I had struggled to get the Wichita office up and selling because they had a tough service manager who thought glass break detectors false-alarmed too much. In reality, he was the one who had to go fix the problems so his concern was valid.

The KC team said, "Don't try to sell Dennis." They further added, "Ask him his opinions and if you just let him stay in charge and talk, you have a shot of converting him over." Isn't that the same advice people give to survive a kidnapper or a killer? Basically the advice was even though he was difficult personality treat him with respect. I did just as advised and Dennis came around and ADT Wichita started to use our BGE9100 dual technology glass break detectors. I remember that sales call very well, because he was a tough cookie and as a young sales guy I was trying a new technique—like giving a fighting fish a lot of line before you try to reel him in.

Fast forward 16 years. I was watching TV in 2005 and news was breaking that the BTK killer in Wichita, Kansas, had been arrested after a 21-year run. I was 90 percent sure I recognized the guy on TV, but he had a really common look, balding guy with a mustache, and who should recognize a serial killer? I had not been in Wichita, Kansas in over a decade. In addition, an old friend named Tim Rader had just moved to Dallas to run product development at Brinks Security. I thought maybe I'm wrong and recognized the last name Rader, and not the face. When you are young, you remember tough defining moments and the converting of the service manager in Wichita always stuck with me.

Googling someone was fairly new at the time, so I jumped out of bed and Googled Dennis Rader and there it was...Dennis Rader worked at ADT from 1974-1988! It still gives me chills writing it now. Sometimes treating everyone with respect could literally come down to life or death.

7

Help Your Way Out of a Slump

Rex Underwood won our car give away with PAR. No more slump for him!

I stole this idea and it works!! Shame on me I don't remember who from (I heard this is what happens when you turn 50). If you are having a bad moment or day, immediately find someone in need and help them! It instantly and 100% of the time snaps you out of your funk! Simple as waiting to hold a door open, donating to someone in need. Go out of your way to say a kind word. Giving someone a lottery ticket snaps you out of your bad mood 100% of the time! I'm not talking later in the week or a month from now. I'm talking the very next instance!

Everyone gets in a bad mood, but the real difference is how fast you get out of that bad mood! It's totally up to you how quick you are back to normal. Can you imagine being a doctor and prescribing this antidepressant that works every time without any side effects like this one little trick? I believe habits both good ones and bad ones define your destiny.

Therefore, I have developed the habit of recognizing early when I'm in a funk and correcting it right away by being charitable to someone less fortunate the second my mood goes negative. Think about it. If you had treatable cancer would you want to remove it the second it appeared in your body or would you want to wait awhile and let it grow and fester? Then why be in a bad mood a second longer than you have to? You control you, so choose to get out of your slump right away, not some other day.

8

Written Goals

My buddies Jim Zadeh, Mike Shirley, Pat Nolan and I write our written goals together.

Set written goals!! And yes they have to be written. Ninety percent of people don't do this one simple act. WRITE YOUR GOALS DOWN! Absolutely changed my life when I first did it when I was 19 years old and still do to this day.

I read a book about the 1953 Yale graduating class members being asked if they had written goals and 5% of the class did. All these bright kids and 95% didn't have written goals. The story goes (and some people now dispute the validity of the story....but it worked for me so I want to believe it was true) that the researchers came back 20 years later and checked to see how the class was doing financially. The 5% with goals collectively were worth more than the 95% put together!

So here I was a 19-year-old kid who just had a roommate up and leave without paying his share of the bills. I went to the apartment manager in Bedford, Texas, and ask if she could help me honor my lease by allowing me to move from the two-bedroom apartment to a one-bedroom efficiency apartment. Lucky for me she helped me out and allowed me to move into the cheaper smaller space. I was very concerned and worried I might struggle to honor this new financial commitment. I promptly had only one thing on my wall—a list of my written goals, with the biggest goal of all to have my rent money in a money order by the 15th of month. Why money order? That way I couldn't play mental games like the money in my checking account. When the money order was made out to Pointe Loma Woods Apartments it wasn't going to be used for anything else.

How my goal list worked was I would spring up from my mattress on the floor (I couldn't afford a frame and box spring at the time) and read all my goals and sign in with the date at the bottom of the page. At nighttime, I would mark the date next to any goal I worked towards achieving that day. By doing that, it became very apparent what I was working on in life and what I wasn't—a long list of dates on certain goals next to nothing on other goals. The thing you learn about goals is it's like sales. It tells you quickly what you are doing right and what you are doing wrong.

The biggest goal at 19 years old was survival and that meant rent in the money order. I was pleasantly surprised at easily achieving my goal of rent by the 15th. All I did was pick up as many waiting table shifts as I could until I had enough money to get the money order for rent. So I challenged myself and moved the goal up from the 15th to the 10th of the month, the very next month. I achieved that and moved the goal again forward, from the 10th to the 5th. Finally, from the 5th then the 3rd! That tough goal only a few months prior became obtainable.

I made a new goal of buying a house by the time I was 20 years old. No one was going to give a mortgage to a 19-year- old back in 1985 (maybe subprime leading years of 2004-2008) so my folks were going to co-sign. I set a new goal of finding a house to buy. Easy, right? In the middle of my search my dad lost his job, thus no cosigner. This wasn't going to stop me. The goal just had to be adjusted. I wasn't going to abandon my goal. The new goal was to find out how I could buy a house without any credit. It took some time back then without the luxury of the Internet. I researched and learned you could assume a VA or FHA loan without a credit check! I reduced my search to just FHA and VA assumable mortgages.

Bingo, I found the perfect little house and I'm in with a small down payment and at 19 years and 10 months I'm a homeowner! My house at 3512 View Street, Fort Worth, Texas, was a red brick, two-bedroom, one-bath, one- car garage home that sat on an acre of land for $45,000. To say that I believe in written goals I do! They have always helped me along my journey! I'm a fan of others having novelty license plates but not for me, that said I have often been tempted to get the plate "SET GLS". I don't reflect much and feel prideful, but to go from living with your parents at 18 years and 6 months old and having your own house 16 short months later is pretty amazing. I doubt it would have happened without written goals, and more importantly actively working those written goals.

9

Rebounding Your Way

to Sales Success

Two guys who made a living rebounding and following up.
One you know as Dennis Rodman. The other is a great
human being named Jason Byrd.

I'm in sales, but I think it's true in all aspects of life. Great follow up is the difference between having what you want in life and not. Most folks in sales don't get to where they want to be in life, and I estimate 80% of sales people don't give extraordinary follow up. Not a coincidence! If it was just present your offer or service and everyone buys, follow up wouldn't be necessary. But we all agree that's not how life is. So if we agree, then let's agree that follow up is extremely important.

My visual for follow up is rebounding in basketball. The sales call is like a shot in basketball, and just like in sales it does go in about 35% of the time. Average basketball game scores would be 31-29 without rebounding. But the reason why games are 100-98 is all the second and third chances because of rebounding. Famous basketball coach and current GM of the Miami Heat Pat Riley has a saying, "No rebounds, no championship rings". The same is true with sales follow-up. "No follow up, no financial freedom!" Just like all the extra sales you get by going back, calling, emailing, staying on the prospect. Show me a successful person without follow-up and I will show you a unicorn, (second unicorn reference is for Brad Sampson) because they are both myths.

Crystal, my lovely wife, started a career in real estate, and she was on the fence about making an additional phone call to a family that was looking to list their home for sale. The family was interviewing four to six other real estate agents. Being a salesman since 21 years old I STRONGLY encouraged her to call the family again. Crystal said she didn't want to "bug" them and that they would call her when they were ready.

After a bit of overbearing nagging on my part, I told her to think happy thoughts and she would probably just get voice mail so zero pressure. I encouraged her to leave a peppy (she exudes peppy 24/7) voicemail, and basically say, "I can't wait to get started and get your lovely home sold for you." She got the real estate listing a few days later, but I'm convinced the extra follow up and really WANTING the opportunity to help them help beat out 4-6 realtors who had bigger names in the community. Never underestimate follow up. It's the difference in achieving your goals and dreams or not. There's a saying "a goal is just a dream, without action." Follow up is the mandatory action for success.

10

Solve Your Way to Success

My friend Chris Roberts from Global and the famous Zig Ziglar.

Solve problems don't create problems. You will make more money and be happier in life by asking customers what their problems are and solving them, than creating problems for them.

I know this sounds elementary, but most people don't solve problems for their clients, let alone go the extra mile and ask the client what they are missing or what challenges they are facing and need help with. I have a great customer who had a giveaway item that was being discontinued. The item was a fire resistant power strip. The power strip was the toy in the "Happy Meal" of their high-dollar smoke detector sale. It was the low cost extra item that helped folks say "yes" to the bigger sale. I tried to source a new fire strip but couldn't get right on price and, more importantly, the attached equipment warranty.

The power strip insured and promised to pay for anything damaged that was plugged into the strip. So the search began for a $10 give away item that made sense to their core business. Most sales reps would walk away and wish them good luck, but I've learned there is money in solving client's challenges. After racking my brain for fire-related items and striking out on price and relevancy, I came up with another item that alerted you when there was trouble in the home: Water damage. Next step was sourcing a water sensor that wasn't on the market, looked like a smoke detector and was very affordable. Because of helping a client I now have a new line of profitable water sensors. But more importantly, I have a much closer friend and customer Chris Roberts, and I'm sure I will get first crack at the next product they are looking to source.

I involved Haylee and Garrett, our kids that we have raised together. I walked them through the sourcing, logo, designing, website, the box, etc. Then I give them 25-cent royalty per unit sold. It taught them about customs, and what our costs and profits are. I'm excited in about three weeks they will receive their largest royalty check yet; $1,250 each! Its exciting teaching them about business and actually having some of that profit go towards their futures! (Update. The kids have now had six royalty checks in less than two years.)

There's no money in NO! If you chose to always pass problems to someone else, realize that someone else will always be paid more money than you. Now if you are the person who can solve problems, minimize problems, or fix problems, you become more valuable. When you add value, you become more valuable. In Chapter 1, I wrote that you would be crazy to think extra should come to you without giving extra effort. The same is true here. If you are constantly passing problems down the line and expect to do better in life, you are fooling yourself. Again in the dictionary, the word solving comes before success, just like it does in life!

11

Multi-task, Multi-income streams

Here are the multiple lines and multiple streams of income from my security business.

Multi-task in life whenever possible. So many folks may say concentrate on one thing. I disagree in regards to sales. It takes the same amount of time to shave, get dressed and go see customers, so you might as well have as many things to create revenue streams!

Perfect example is my friend Jeremy, who sells medical supplies to doctors' offices. His job is a corporate job with great pay and benefits. He wanted to create an additional way to make money. So Jeremy worked into the conversation with the office administrator that he has great friends who are in the promotional products business and if she wasn't just totally happy with who she is using would you mind if Bobbi Jo or Ashlee from GoLogo gives you a call. What does Jeremy get? He gets a new revenue stream of 5% override on that account forever. Does Jeremy know how much a pen or shirt cost? No. Did it conflict or distract from his current job? No. I would argue that it makes him more motivated to call on more doctors' office now that he has more ways to get paid. He has a wife and kids to feed!

Jeremy was going to talk to the office administrator about something, might as well have been about something he could make money for. The great thing about Jeremy is the reason why he wants to make the extra money? He wants it to pay for Dallas Cowboys season tickets to take his kids. He feels like that's a luxury his regular money isn't intended for. With his multi-tasking money, he feels no guilt. Who wins by multitasking? Jeremy's corporate job because he's more motivated to see more doctors' offices. The doctor office wins because they are going to save money and get better promo gear. Jeremy family wins because they have more time together and would be doing a fun activity together. GoLogo wins because they got another account.

Maybe I wouldn't multi-task if I was selling Lear Jets. Maybe that would be a big enough sale that I might say just focus on the jet. Or maybe I would be seriously tempted to sell jet insurance, sell or lease them a hangar to park their jet in, sell an extended warranty or a vacation home to fly the jet to. Offer them a detailing service to clean their plane, find them a pilot and flight attendant to help onboard the plane. Suggest a pet sitter or home sitter while they are on vacation. There are eight examples of very logical ways of creating additional revenue streams while selling a high-end item like a jet. Through the years, it just has made sense to try to sell multiple items to our clients. A steak restaurant sells steaks, right? But they also sell mashed potatoes, asparagus, and drinks to wash it all down. Then later sell them a gift card to get you to come back again! Here's how I see it. They are going to buy "blank" it might as well be from us!

In my core business, security representation, I love that at any given time we have 25 to 30 different lines to sell to alarm and audio visual companies. Then add to that, our seven financial services and finish it off with GoLogo, which can produce all logo shirts, pens, caps, etc. If I have any empty rent house at the time, I'm going to try to place someone in one of our investment properties at a more than fair deal. If someone is in need of a home to buy, like new friend Dan Fitzgerald from Central Station Marketing, I'm going to refer them to Crystal to help them buy a home, which Dan did with his lovely wife, Siobhan. Remember it took the same amount of effort to go see that client whether you sold him one thing or 21 things. The hidden gem is the more you do, the more important you are to your client. The deeper and more important the bond will be for both of you. In my mind, being more helpful to a customer actually turns them into a lifelong friend. I'm no longer Tim the sales guy of a widget; I'm Tim their trusted friend.

Multitasking is a faster way to be financially successful and to build stronger more important relationships. You are leveraging your time with the ability to offer multiple services. One of the first financial goals of many driven young men is to make $100,000 in one year. Every person who has made $100K can tell you three things: what company they were working for, who their boss was and how old they were.

For me it was IntelliSense/Ben Cornett/1993 and I was 28 years old. Like every daunting task, I like to reduce it into bite size pieces. If you want to work a normal amount of hours (40 hour

48

work week) and make $100,000 you need to make $48.08 an hour. That's it! $48.08 times 40 hours times 52 weeks is a hair over $100K. That's why you need to multi-task, multi-line and leverage your time. Very few build wealth in a timely manner without leverage.

12

Leverage

Nathan and Josh Randall and Pat Nolan, the King of Leverage

LEVERAGE is one of the best words in the English language. I love this word. I see examples of leverage every day. My buddy Clay Conn and I always talk about leverage when we catch up. Clay is one of my few friends who actively looks for examples of leverage everywhere. I didn't understand leverage, what it meant, how to use it, and how it was used against me until I was about 35 years old. I read about how virtually every great fortune was made with leverage and without leverage you had to have a monumental moment happen or live to be 100 to gain a financial windfall.

Leverage in a tool form allows you to lift, carry, and remove more than you should be able to. Visualize a board with a pivot point lifting a huge boulder on the other end that you couldn't lift on your own. Here's that same image in a financial form. My favorite use of leverage is with real estate. I love that you can put a 20% down payment on a rental house and the bank puts up 80%. So your little 20% allowed you to pick up (obtain) this huge 100% ownership (or control) of a rental property. With leverage you get a house today verses waiting 10-15 or even 30 years to finally have saved enough money to pay cash for that rental house. The sad thing is that the house would typically cost you more now that you waited, like chasing a leaf in the wind.

Another way of thinking about it is this example. Let's say you do have $100K and a rent house that you want to buy is $100K. So without leverage you buy one rent house with your $100K. No leverage but nice safe investment. Now apply leverage, the power to lift or do more than you can by taking that same $100K but using five chunks of $20K and buying 5- $100K houses. You own 20% of five houses and the bank owns 80%. Now fast forward 15 years and those $100K houses are now worth $200K each. In the non-leverage example, your one paid for house is worth $200K—a nice 100% increase; your $100K turned into $200K and you don't owe anyone anything. Now in the leveraged five house example, those five houses are worth $200K each or $1 million. You put $20K down on each of the houses with a starting mortgage of $80K.

Now 15 years later, let's say you owe $50K on each house; all the while your renters have been paying off your mortgage for you. Let's assume the renters have covered the mortgages plus a little profit. Let's tally up what the leveraged five house example is worth: you still owe the bank 5X$50K = $250K minus $1 million value. So with leverage you have $750K net value verses the non-leveraged $200K one house example – same time period but more than three times the value.

I thank my friend Pat Nolan (owner of Advantage Protection and 10 locations of Self Storage) for explaining leverage to me. Pat is a totally self-made guy who is married to Amy. Pat owned an alarm company and he and Amy used the equity in that business to borrow (leverage) and open their first self-storage business. They then continued to borrow against their current storage facility to build their next facilities. What Pat taught me was that if one house in a great area is good then 10 would be better! Pat asked questions like, "Do you think the U.S. dollar will be more or less valuable in the future?" I, of course, answered less valuable! Pat then replied then why in the world do you want to pay rentals properties off early with good "today dollars" when you could pay that mortgage off later with less valuable "tomorrow dollars?" You have more properties and more money because you aren't busy paying down on the few properties you have.

Pat also said he was amazed when he went to self-storage conventions, how many independent storage owners only had one facility. Pat said they would talk fondly of how their one facility was a great investment and they were glad they had that facility. I love how simply my friend Pat sees things. He makes business look easy by simply repeating and recreating things that work over and over again! Sure enough, Pat hit his goal of 10 facilities in 2015. He and Amy use the value of the other facilities to borrow money from the banks to build the next facility, so literally they are building additional sites without any extra dollars coming out of their pockets. Without Pat's insight and guidance I would have acquired rentals slowly. I would have maybe half the houses I have in the great city of Southlake. Finding affordable houses in that great school district is extremely hard, and now every good house comes with a bidding war. If an affordable house comes up for sale, it has 10 offers and is gone in a day. This may be bad for me as a buyer, but amazingly good for me as an eventual seller. Once I understood what Pat was doing. It gave me great confidence to go A LOT faster and use leverage to my financial advantage.

Throughout the process of rapidly acquiring rental properties, I would call my great friend and attorney Jim Zadeh. Jim is extremely level headed and a great sounding board. I would ask Jim if I was going too fast, he would ask me pointed questions, and we came to the conclusion that I wasn't going too fast. I mentioned earlier that I see leverage everywhere, in relationships, business dominance, etc. An example of business leverage would be Walmart over the manufacturers of products that they sell. Let's say you make straws to drink soda with, and you sell through Walmart. Walmart can sell a zillion of your straws, so you are forced to acknowledge their dominance and give them the best price best terms and best delivery.

Walmart owns all the leverage or advantage in the relationship because there are 25 other straw manufactures that would love to be in your shoes. You are forced to acknowledge that if you lose Walmart business there isn't anywhere to make it up. I have a saying that I use weekly, if not daily. "The person bitching doesn't have the leverage." What I mean by that is if someone is complaining about something I bet there's 99% chance that person doesn't have the leverage or upper hand in the relationship or scenario.

For example, you complain that yet again the price of a stamp has gone up! Post office holds all the leverage because no one is going to deliver anything 2000 miles away for only 53 cents, so bitch all you want they hold all the cards. With my business and rental properties I don't abuse the position, I hold with leverage but I sure do enjoy being on the lever side more than de-lever side. There's an old saying that goes: the real golden rule is the one with the gold makes the rules. The same could be said with leverage, "the one with the leverage makes the rules."

15 Years Later
January 1st, 2032
NO LEVERAGE

$100K HOUSE
YOU OWN 100%

**NOW WORTH
$200K
YOU MADE
$100K**

LEVERAGE

HOUSE #1	HOUSE #2	HOUSE #3	HOUSE #4	HOUSE #5

$20K DOWN	$20K DOWN	$20K DOWN	$20K DOWN	$20K DOWN
$50K LOAN	$50K LOAN	$50K LOAN	$50K LOAN	$50K LOAN
100% CONTROL	100% CONTROL	100% CONTROL	100% CONTROL	100% CONTROL
WORTH $200K	WORTH $200K	WORTH $200K	WORTH $200K	WORTH $200K
$150K EQUITY	$150K EQUITY	$150K EQUITY	$150K EQUITY	$150K EQUITY

$ 1 MILLION VALUE
YOU OWE $250K
YOU MADE
5 x $150K = $750K

13

1 in 98 shot to 1 Million

**My stepson Garrett at around 6-7, dressed up and took a
selfie.**

Look for the different way of thinking or doing things. I just saw the statistic that 98.6% of Americans will never have a net worth of over $1 million (excludes equity in home). That means that if your goal is to be a millionaire, which I had when I was a little boy after getting kicked underneath the table at brunch, you will most likely need to align yourself with successful people as soon as you can. Secondly you need to not conform with and not do what the norm is, i.e., what the 98% tell you to do.

I did just this when I was 32 years old. I walked away from a corporate job paying almost $140K, company car, 401K and expense account in 1997. ($207K in 2015 dollars) Why? Because I knew (well, I hoped I knew) that conforming was never going to get me where I wanted to go, and for sure not fast enough. Secondly, having one line of products and signing a huge non-compete that included verbiage like "anything I think of is their idea document" wasn't the right thing for me. It might be the right thing for safety conscious people, but I had bigger goals and a quicker timeline in mind. When you walk away from that much security, it's an all-in bet on yourself.

I read somewhere that the word JOB was an acronym for "Just over Broke." A job keeps you just satisfied enough to keep going on. With my companies I always have ways for employees to make more money; I want them to make more! I have cut employees in on real estate deals and am willing to help with their personal goals. Align yourself with successful and moral people willing to help you achieve your goals.

14

You Bet

I might have lost money on my investment, but I won big time by hiring the best guy that worked there! Kyle Seay a superstar at PAR.

My old friend Lance Dean (co-founder of www.2gig.com and www.encorecontrols.com) and I laugh at this point. It seems as if we both have many examples of how we do well when we bet on ourselves—or at least we know who to blame—and that it is almost a guaranteed loss when we hand money to someone else. Restaurants, financial planners, stock brokers, dreamers and schemers. I invested $25K in a restaurant in nearby Southlake, Texas, and right out of the chute the guy running it started using the place as his personal piggy bank. My first clue that this was not going to work was when he decided the place should be named after him! The second clue was when I was willing to sell my shares two months into the deal for half off at $12,500. He wasn't interested in buying them, but he was curious why I would be willing to lose that much. I told him if I could recoup 50% I could use that money to make up the loss over a period of time. He missed the first two shareholder payments, and I was sure my investment would go zero under his non-watchful eye. It did.

Was I or am I mad? Absolutely not, it was a valuable lesson. Am I mad at the person that had his name on the restaurant? Absolutely not, in his mind he believed he could do it! But you don't want minority interest in investments, and you want to be able to do what you need to do to turn a tough situation around. You can't do that when you have very little say in your investment. I read this question awhile back, and I love it! When deciding to invest in something ask yourself, "Is this your dream or their dream you are investing in?" If it's someone else's dream, make sure you have a clear path to getting your money back or how you can create a revenue stream. An estimated 50% of businesses fail in the first five years. I feel that you have far more control and a better chance of success when you bet on yourself.

15

Help Friends Find Jobs

Ernest Bernard and my wonderful dog Trixie. Ernest is so
amazingly talented, always has a top-tier job and doesn't
need help. Sometimes, a kind word or a nudge can always
help a decision-maker pick the obvious right choice.

A theme of a relationship book I recently read was that women find their self-worth in the quality of their relationships while men find their self-worth in their work. I equate a man losing a job to a woman losing a best friend. It can be devastating. According to PBS, men are twice as likely to commit suicide when not holding a job. Not surprisingly, the number is higher the older the man. Someone who loses his job after 20-30 years is a prime target to take his own life, but may be the least likely guy to do the unthinkable.

If you would have asked me 20 years ago who would be in my Top 10 most together guy, this guy was in it. He was a top producer at Northwestern Mutual Insurance, a master of referrals and world class follow up. He started to do worse and worse at work, and, sure enough, the guy we all thought had it together took his own life. Similar situation with another friend, so always lend a hand to an unemployed or struggling friend. I have two sad examples, plus a fake-death-and-flee-the-country story. The fake death story is in Chapter 45.

So, I help anyone (from a lifetime friend to an acquaintance) when they are fired or without a job. I take it as seriously as if they were about to commit suicide. I don't half-ass it. I don't just give them one potential job opportunity. I give them as many as they need until they get a job. I don't call once. I check back, and then check again. I look for an opportunity and call the potential head-hunter or employer. I talk about the person's strong qualities or good character. Then I follow up (Those words again). My work is not over until they have a job. I try to call on Monday mornings because that's when you start your week and the unemployed don't have a place to go. A benefit of finding someone in need of a job is the good karma and the feeling that you are doing something for the greater good.

It is extremely rewarding helping someone in need. During my 50 years, I have probably helped 40 to 50 folks get a job. Recently, I helped a friend get to the next step on an interview, and another friend, Chancy Pray, thanked me at a trade show for the kind words to the company that had just hired him. Some remember that I helped them, and some don't. Some will do business with me in their new job, and some will never contact me again. It doesn't matter! I remember when my father was without a job for the first time in his life in his 50s. He came from an era where you worked at a job for 40 years and retired with a gold watch. The world changed in the 1980s with leverage buyout and junk bonds, companies were gutted, and the generation of guys expecting job security were kicked to the curb. That event changed my father, and it changed me too. I saw what it does to a man to not be able to provide, to have someone think they are better off without you. It hurts and when my friends are hurting I step up! I will continue finding jobs for people until the day I die. It's that important.

16

Give Referrals

**John Rose, head hunter extraordinaire, and marketing genius
Keith Marshall and me in 2015**

I think by now you realize that I'm proud to say that I'm a professional salesman. My old boss, Ben, used to say nothing happens until something is sold. He is right! What he meant by that is something needs to be sold, so the factory can make the widget and the factory workers get paid, the factory pays their utility bills, the folks at the utility company get paid, they can now go buy cars and houses and on and on. By Ben saying that to me at a young age it did two things. One, it made me proud of my profession and, two, it made realize that I have a lot of responsibility to be the best salesman I could be because all sales folks have a responsibility to create opportunity for non-sales people. Don't get me wrong. I'm not putting sales people above doctors, teachers, and any other noble profession. Think about the new car business. If cars aren't selling, the auto maker shuts down production and all those workers are without jobs. Lack of sales has a large, negative trickle down effect.

I prefer to live in America when the economy is humming along verses depression, recession, and general upheaval. Maybe most people don't think this way but I consciously think every day that I have to be a positive influence on the economy and not a negative. I need to create more than I take. There's an old saying in golf, you repair your divot in the grass plus one other, and I believe the same thing with regards to helping the economy. Do your part and then some more. I have addressed how I encourage every positive person in my path, I tip extremely well, and I tip virtually every one I come in contact with, whether it's a kind word, money, lotto ticket, or giving them a treat. Recently, I took my Tesla in for service and along with two dozen Krispy Kreme donuts. Boy were they surprised and happy!

The ultimate treat is referrals. I love referring customers to people who sell a product or service that they are looking for. Just this morning, I referred my buddy Bill McNabney's friend Deacon to look at two potential roofing jobs on my rent houses. Sometimes people think that they can't positively influence a huge issue or situation, like the economy. I disagree. You can help the economy every day by looking to hook people up with services and products that you like.

Writing this book has been a joyous ride and while writing this chapter about referrals I was flying back from a convention in Jacksonville with Crystal and about five to six guys from the security industry. My boss on our wildly successful stereo speaker line, Keith Marshall (www.proficientaudio.com) grabbed me out of my seat and introduced me to Jeff Smith, who's sitting next to him 15 rows away. Jeff runs three great companies from chocolate to hamburgers. Keith Marshall realized that Jeff would be a great lead for our promotional products business, GoLogo and got me an introduction! Literally what I've been writing happened! Keith wanted us to be successful, and I wanted the same for him!! So what did Keith do? He referred business! So if you think the economy can be better then make it better by referring people to other good people. If you are lucky enough to be a salesman, refer business to other salespeople. It will always come back to you!

17

Three Way Calls

Golfing with the king of three way calls, Lance Dean.

I learned this from Lance Dean (Co-founder of 2GIG and great friend) amazingly few people use this great tool; I use it 5-25 times a day! Thank you Apple and AT&T! I taught my friend Mark O'Keefe how to do it! So a client called and asked me a question, but I didn't know the answer. Years ago I would have hung up, called the folks who might have the answers, perhaps would have left a message with a receptionist or on voicemail and waited for a call back. When I got the answer, I would have called back the client with the initial question and relayed the information, probably at 80% as good as the person who gave me the answer. But more times than not the client would have had a follow-up question or two and I would have had to start the process all over. All this took time and you learned less than in an interactive conversation. Scratch all that.

In three way calls, (sometimes four-way) you get the person with the question and the people with the answers. Everyone wins! Inquirer gets an accurate and quick answer. The person answering the question feels important, wanted, needed, and receives the joy of helping. I learn information because I'm listening on the call, so hopefully the next time I can answer the question on my own. The bonus is this information exchange took considerably less time than leaving messages, email, text, and multiple returned calls for everyone involved. Added bonus is that the person who called got world-class service. Will they keep buying your goods and services? You bet! You now have more time, to sell, and help more people. On an iPhone, while you are on a call look at lower left corner, there is a "plus" symbol. Hit that and another person then you will see a merge symbol and that combines all three people. I stole this great business idea from Lance Dean and what a heist it was. Use it EVERY day, if not every hour of every day!

18

Don't Beautiful Barbara Things

Don't wait around wishing and dreaming. My lovely wife waiting for Garrett at his 7th grade birthday party at Six Flags over Texas in 2015.

I had a shack of a rental property on the most prestigious street in a really affluent, never-going-to-go-backwards-in-value, town of Southlake, Texas. The challenge was my lot was shaped like the state of Oklahoma put on its side. So the panhandle (skinny part) located on that great street called White Chapel. The wider part was farther away from the street. The shack of a house I called the Unabomber Shack, brought in a modest amount of rent, but it was truly a land play with its wooded 1.4 acres. So having this quirky shaped lot made me want to buy some land from my neighbors to create a better shaped lot. Striking out with the two neighbors that could make Oklahoma look like Kansas and square the lot up I looked to my neighbor to the left, my last chance... Barbara! Barbara was my last chance and after striking out with the two other neighbors I knew I HAD to make it work with Barbara (If you are expecting a happy ending, eliminate that thought from your mind now). So Barbara was a career flight attendant in the golden age of flying. She went through a divorce two decades ago and stayed in shape by gardening every day! She had more than three acres of land and being over 65 I'm thinking that she would welcome the opportunity to make some money and lower her property to take care of. I mean a nice little payday by selling off a slice of her property would really help with a flight attendant pension...right?! WRONG. And not only wrong but because this was my last chance to get more land on a great street in a great town, guess what I did?

I took over a year and half of visiting with her talking to her before I declared my intentions. All the while dreaming of the big house I would build and spread out nicely on the extra acre that I was going to buy at a fair price from Barbara. Just like the guy that's scared to put his arm around the girl in the theater he starts, stops, acts like he's yawning, it took an eternity for me to make Barbara an offer. All the while not taking the obvious clues (and you call yourself a salesman?) that her yard is her life! Her yard is literally keeping her fit, so trying to buy a piece of it was like cutting off an arm but giving her a $100K for it! The day came when I gave Barbara a written offer to show her I was serious. I had been dreaming about this for 500 days so I really knew what I wanted to say and how I wanted to say it! Did Barbara get worked up when she got my offer?! You bet she did!! She was speechless... no literally wouldn't return my calls! Barbara was so insulted by my offer both monetarily and that I was coveting her land for the last 500 days, that she made it clear the price would be double before she would EVEN consider. Sooo.... I never bought the land. Promptly put my lot up for sale since I was land-locked and Oklahoma shaped lots aren't the most desirable shape.

Fortunately, made a 75% profit, still a great street and an even better town. The lesson to learn is don't "beautiful Barbara" a situation. To this day when I catch myself stalling, wishing, dreaming and hoping someone will accept an offer that I haven't presented, I immediately pull my head out of the clouds and make an offer, make the call and stop "Beautiful Barbara-ing it."

19

Dialing for Dollars

My good friend Scott Crown at the spot in Dallas where JFK
was assassinated. Scott is a world-class communicator.

In sales, call, don't text, if you are a good communicator. Here's a news flash that took me a long while to realize. You interpret a text with your current mood. The same text when you are happy reads in a good way; if you are upset it reads in a bad way. If you are a poor communicator or have bad social skills then utilize email and text to your benefit. If you are a cheerful, happy, funny, fun person by all means grab the phone and let the person on the other line hear your joy and excitement!

I get it that there are times when a text is the right way to respond, but I look for the marginal times where a call will be a better form of communication. Even if you get voice mail, you are better off leaving a cheerful voicemail than a potentially misunderstood text. I'm an optimistic contrarian, which means that I'm a very positive person, but I love to look at doing things the opposite or contrarian way. So if the world is text happy, then that means the vintage way of communicating might be the place you want to be.

Just last night, I saw a Vintage Led Zeppelin and then a Rolling Stones T-shirt on EBay, both in excess of $250! Why? It's because they aren't making any more authentic vintage T-shirts. Just like those vintage items going up in value so will your value with doing the contrarian ways of communicating like calling and written mailed notes. The more you communicate, the more opportunity. The most successful people in business I know seem like they are always on the phone. Back in the day, you had to use pay phones with calling cards, because cell phone minutes were extremely expensive.

I recall I was at DFW airport, and my flight was delayed. Instead of reading a magazine or doing some other time wasting activity I used the delay to grab a pay phone and call customers to both try to sell products, as well as set future appointments. I get a call on my cell phone from my boss Ben, who asks, "Is everything ok?" I said, "Yes". He asked if I was in possession of my phone calling card and I told him I was. Thinking nothing more of the event I went back to banging out more customer touches. A few months later all the salesmen for IntelliSense were brought into Louisville, Ky., and we had a meeting. Ben, always the master of complimenting one person while trying to motivate others, told a story in front of us all. Ben has amazing delivery when speaking to a group. He told how an AT&T fraud person called him, because of the intense activity on a calling card at DFW Airport. I love that I was cranking out so many customer calls that it tripped fraud alert. Ben used it as an example of hustle when you have adversity like a flight delay. In closing, there isn't a substitute for activity in business, make the extra call, make the extra connection. Everyone has adversity. Make it an opportunity.

20

Solutions, No Dump Trucks

Man in Hartford, Ky., found a solution to his challenge of mowing on a hill.

We have a rule in our businesses. If you come with problems, you must come to me with solutions, too. I hate the word problem; I prefer to think of a problem as a challenge or an opportunity to grow a relationship, or help someone, sometimes yourself. We will call it a challenge for this conversation. I'm not sure when we instituted this in our businesses; perhaps, it was at least 12 years ago. As your business or responsibilities grow, more people will come to you with challenges. What I noticed is the relief in the person when they "dumped" a challenge at my feet. Well, when you have multiple businesses and a lot going on you start to get a stack of challenges real quick. The biggest concern with challenge dumping is that the people dumping challenges aren't learning anything by dumping.

Think about this. If you do your kids homework for them and don't teach them how to solve their homework, what have they really learned? Just like doing a child's homework, in business when you allow people to dump challenges at your feet, you can guarantee they will be back to dump more on you. The folks I work with are sharper and smarter than me on tons of issues, but they thought I needed to make the decision to all challenges. If I continued to make all the decisions three things wouldn't grow: their knowledge, my knowledge, and our business! I explained from that point forward, please feel free to come to me with challenges, but you have to bring a few solutions too. Simple as that, you bring challenges but they have to be accompanied with possible solutions. The amazing thing happened; a lot less challenges showed up at my feet and when they did, the challenge was more than half solved, mostly because we went with one of their solutions to solve the challenge. It was great to see the number of challenges diminished, but even better seeing how folks I work with were growing personally.

There's another hidden gem in this thinking. If someone is part of the solution they are really behind that solution. If they weren't involved in the solution there are various levels of acceptance in the solution. Now that it's their solution, they explain it better to the customer; they feel better about the resolution, and we get that challenge turned around much faster.

74

Just recently with GoLogo, we accidentally shipped some promo gear to the wrong office about 175 miles away from each other in California. Ashlee called and said the customer was asking us what we could do to compensate them for the two-and-a-half-hour drive to retrieve the gear from the wrong office. Ashlee came to me with a solution. We then added another solution so our very good client could pick their resolution to the challenge. Ashlee came to me with "can we compensate their driver $250 to pick up the gear (its California)?" My concern was they might not order again, and we lose a client. I offered a second solution for Ashlee to offer a $500 credit. The client took the $500 credit, which I'm thrilled because that means we had a misunderstanding, but they will be back.

As a business owner, I am happy that the client picked the remedy that best satisfied them. I've often thought that one of the main differentiators between successful people and those who aren't where they want to be in life is the ability to solve more challenges. Finally, problems are only challenges, and when you properly overcome a challenge more times than not great opportunity awaits you.

21

Don't leave your Success to Chance

Bringing Lotto Tickets to my favorite people who work at the world class steak house Pappas Brothers Dallas, Texas, on 12/21/2015, my 50th Birthday.

I carry Lotto tickets at all times. When I started writing this book I would jot down an idea for one of the 50 ideas and nine times out of 10 I wouldn't write about that subject; then I would go back and write about that concept at a later time. I once was on an SWA flight from Dallas to Los Angeles with a stop in lovely Albuquerque. The flight I was on was two hours late from our departure city of Dallas. A rare event for the great Southwest Airlines! So I was writing on a few of my items in this book and now somewhere over Arizona I see number No. 21: Carry lotto tickets. Two thoughts came to mind. Anyone who knows me knows that you have a better chance of me wearing two shoes that don't match than not having Lotto tickets on me. My second thought is that 21 is my favorite number, and this is one of my favorite things I choose to do. I'm glad fate created No. 21 to be "Carry Lotto tickets!"

So the plane was late and being 14 days before Christmas, SWA gate agents offered a $25 travel voucher (don't you love the Herb Kelleher culture?!) to any passenger that was willing to grab the PA at the gate and sing a Christmas Carol! This happy lady did just that and I quietly slipped her a Lotto ticket and said great job! She loved it! More fate, the singer sat across the row from me and we were visiting about her guts to sing in front of 300-400 people who gave her a roaring ovation. Coincidentally, I videoed her singing and she was super excited to get that forwarded to her to share with her fiancé.

Meanwhile, a nice male flight attendant (equal opportunity Lotto giver) brought me a drink and I slid him a Lotto ticket because he was also two hours late and still had a great attitude! Here's a secret: flight attendants get paid like $3 an hour on the ground so when you are late that sucks, but when you are getting paid one-third of minimum wage and late, that really, really sucks! So if you have a pocket full of Lotto tickets it gives you the amazing gift of radically changing moods for $1! I have been handing them out every day since the Texas Lotto started in 1991. This is just the example of that day. Earlier, on the same day, a humming happy-to-be-at-work lady who gave me a Diet Coke at a

Sonic drive-thru got a ticket with the comment from me of "I love your attitude".

When I arrived in a hurry to the airport, the very polite guy at Love Field Airport Valet quickly explained the great service that he was working for and upgraded me to the top of the line car wash. He got a Lotto ticket too! You could tell the $5 tip was great, but the Lotto ticket made his day! And that's was just in one day! Every day is a great day with scratch-off Lotto tickets in my pocket. Try it. You will be amazed at the response and the ability to change moods for just a buck! McDonalds Dollar Menu has nothing on me; they might temporarily nourish your body for $1, I nourish the soul for $1!

22

Mistakes and Failures Mandatory

Tim's freshman year in high school. Nobody was betting on
me.

Funny that when I was first starting out in life, no one gave me a chance and everyone doubted I could do well. I relished that role. I literally had a 7th-grade teacher tell me I would end up a bum. I like being the underdog more than the favorite any day of the week! The crazy thing is once you start to steadily achieve some successes people start to think you have the Midas touch and that everything you do magically works out for you. Now the guy no one would bet on now is the favorite?! I guess I always was determined to do well and always had a strong sense of self that I would never give up on myself or my dreams. So I get asked this question a lot: Have you ever made a mistake or mistakes? It always catches me off-guard, because someone might perceive me as someone who hasn't screwed up or failed. I normally reply with how much time you got?!

My list of mistakes is a mile long; I'm not in some special mistake-free club. When I was younger, I would hide and really dwell on my mistakes. Fortunately, through the love of reading biographies and business books, I learned that everyone makes mistakes. An amazing number of really great business people have made huge mistakes. This changed my outlook and attitude to past mistakes and when I currently am making mistakes. I embrace my mistakes and value the knowledge I learned from them. An amazing thing happened along the way.

I started noting that if really successful people trust you, they will share their failures openly and candidly! It's really ass-backward that you almost have to be open and honest about your failures and mistakes to achieve a decent level of success. It's as if you hid your failures, you can't achieve. I've read about Ray Kroc (founder of McDonald's) almost losing it all and having to go back to his vendors for some help to keep McDonalds afloat, along with the story (not sure if it's true, but BET it is) about Herb Kelleher, founder of Southwest Airlines, making a mistake and literally going to Vegas to gamble to make payroll or the airline was going to go out of business.

Reading and hearing these stories made me realize it's just part of the process and there is zero way around missing out on the mistakes and failures. In fact, the folks that refuse to make a mistake will never succeed. Let me say that again. Trying to eliminate all mistakes will stunt your success growth. I communicate in my businesses that it's OK to make mistakes and fail. I expect it, to get to where we need to go in our businesses. If later you find it's a mistake, embrace it and let everyone know what we did wrong, what we learned and how we can avoid the same thing in the future!

My great boss, Ben Cornett, used to say, "Make a decision, any decision, and we will either learn from it, or our decision will be right but, either way, we win by making that decision now." Keeping a failure my dirty little secret will only ensure that we will repeat it and by not sharing it with my business friends they may suffer the same fate!

Another story, I was sitting with a buddy of mine and a wealthy friend of his. At the time, these guys are worth more than $20 million liquid and I was still trying to put a few businesses together. This was back when I embraced failure on a scale of 1 to 10 at about a 4 (I'm a 10 now). My buddy, let's call him Joe, doesn't like attention.. Joe always loved having deep soul-searching business conversation, which as a young guy I loved from someone doing so well. Well, Joe asked me when had I really been scared and thought I really had failed.

At that point there were two monumental failures that rattled around in my brain on a regular basis. First was my divorce of 10 years to Elaine. It really bothered me that I couldn't make my marriage work. It bothered me that I made a vow to God and because I wasn't happy and she wasn't either, we got divorced. Secondly, I bought a house when I was 20, then I bought a second house at 21. I assumed a mortgage and because I was young and didn't have extra money I didn't have a professional inspection of the house. The house was pretty and we managed to make payments. The challenge was it had a plumbing problem that just wasn't fixable even if you had money, which I didn't.

I called Chevy Chase Bank who the mortgage was with and tried to work something out to delay payments so I could somehow fix the house. They weren't willing to work with us and I made the conscious decision to abandon the house. I wasn't used to quitting, losing, or walking from a challenge, but I was literally living on top of a cesspool. The other out was to trick someone else to take over payments on the house but being a big believer in karma I didn't want to stick the next guy like the previous owners stuck me.

So now it was Joe's turn. This guy's living in a $5 million house in 2002 dollars and had just sold his half of his business for $16 million. So when he started off by saying almost monthly he and his brother would look at what they could liquidate in their business so they could pay off creditors and just move on. I'm like, "Joe, we're talking about the $16 million, your cut (other brother got $16 million, too) business?" He said, "Yes, we just wanted out. We thought the walls were coming in on us tons of times!"

This candid conversation made me realize that every business, every person makes mistakes. The real key how do you handle it mentally? Embrace it or hide it and it's truly backwards you think to hide to be successful but reality is open up and learn from them, don't dwell and charge on! If I focused on the foreclosure at 22 years old I wouldn't have 158 rentals now! If I focus on the failure of my divorce I wouldn't be in the best relationship of my life now with Crystal!

23

School Always in Session

When I graduated Downers Grove South High School in 1984, I set a goal at graduation that I would only come back for my 10-year reunion if I was well on my way to being successful. In 1994 with my Acura NSX at Downers Grove, Illinois.

If you had told the 16 year old version of me that I would be saying, "read books," I would be thinking there was a 10- speed bicycle accident that must have occurred on my paper route and I hit my head! Here's the thing, I heard this saying and I agree that "the only difference between the today version of you and the one year later version of you is two things, the people you meet and the books that you read. You can substitute the word books with positive written information that you gain via others' experience, expertise, and knowledge. That's it"! It's the people you meet and the knowledge you choose to gain.

Ever since I was young, I viewed myself as the single biggest asset I own. I don't mean that arrogantly. I mean that as I need to always invest in my knowledge. When you grow up middle class or lower, you get a gift. The gift is you know you aren't going to inherit any money and you know, "If it's going to be it's up to me." If I invest in myself it will pay dividends; if I don't I will get paid like a very common commodity. Why do some jobs pay very little? It's because anyone can do the job. Why do some people get paid extremely well? Because they have a rarer skill set. This is simple economics of supply and demand. Therefore, invest in yourself; turn the coal you started out with into a magnificent diamond. I have always been willing to invest in books, seminars, anything that could make me better.

At times folks ask me why do I see something from that angle or how did you come to see something that way? I nicely ask them how many books they have read in their lifetime? Nearly 80% of the time it's zero to 5. Well, if you aren't gaining knowledge outside of what you know, and who you know, you have formed self-imposed limitations. One night, I read 37 quotes from Ray Kroc and learned that his first deal with the McDonalds brothers almost broke him until he started buying the land underneath the McDonalds franchisee and leasing it back to guarantee a positive revenue stream. Here, Mr. Kroc was changing the landscape of the fast-food industry and was going broke until he altered his course slightly.

I always have a few books that I'm reading at any given time. I'm not expecting a life-altering event when I read, just a good idea or two that I can start to implement in my life. Compound that with hundreds of other good ideas do that for 50-70 years and see the results!

A lot like the compounding effect on a lump of coal that can turn into a diamond. Think about it, every lump of coal has the same opportunity as every other lump of coal to turn into a diamond, BUT that lump of coal must put itself in the right situation to turn into a diamond. My boss for our home theatre speaker line, Keith Marshall, made a deal with me that he would give me $2,000 worth of speakers if I sent Ernie Quintana (the most loyal, best partner that I've ever had the pleasure to work with) and Jason Byrd (who now co-owns Security Data Supply in Houston and a great human being) my outside guys at the time to Karrass Negotiation school.

This school travels around the U.S. and it's a two-day course. Keith said I will compensate you for your guys' admission but you have to pay for yourself. I've seen the Karrass ads in airline magazines for years, but Dr. Karrass looked mean and I thought I don't want to be a mean negotiation guy. In addition, I thought I was a good negotiator because I was a salesman. I was wrong on both accounts! I went to the class and learned that the now-deceased Dr. Karrass was a sweetheart of a man and I wasn't nearly as good of a negotiator as I thought I was. The class was a blast and I strongly recommend you invest $1K in yourself.

The single greatest lesson I learned from class was that both sides of a deal has pressure points. My goal was to make that $1K back in a week and I did when I negotiated a sprinkler system on one of my rent properties, down by exactly $1,000. I bet I've made or saved $500K in the last 6 years since the class. What I learned is to understand that the other person, whether you are a buyer or seller they have a set of issues. In America everyone negotiates super-fast compared to rest of the world. So being a hyper-person, I now consciously slow things down. People always say, let's meet in the middle. I used to think that was a good idea.

Now I've learned it's a starting point to negotiate further up or down, depending if I'm the buyer or seller. What I realize is that I missed out on millions by not taking this class when I was in my 20s. I strongly encourage you to take the class and please don't look at it as a $1K expense. If I said to you give me $1K and I will give you a skill that make you $100K or $1M would you give me the $1K? One of the best investments I ever have made in myself. School is always in session for me.

24

Happy Bombs

**Dennis Dop and I celebrating a great year. Sent this picture
to him right after that night. Great little happy Bomb!**

Original idea here. I've stolen a bunch of other ones, but this one is an original! Love happy bombs, kind of a crazy word but been calling them that for so long it would be like changing your dog's name when it turns 10 years old!

When I was a young sales guy in early 1990, I was super active in sending out thank you notes. I had a competitor who inherited a great territory with a ton of commission dollars occurring monthly. He was lazy and coincidently sleeping with a girl that lived three doors down from the townhouse I lived in Fort Worth, Texas. Often times I would be walking out of my home with a handful of hand-written thank you notes, gifts, and other follow-up items to be mailed that day. While my major competitor was still in bed, I was off to go see more people to sell more gear. One day it dawned on me that in two to three days all those letters, gifts, and notes were going to go off in customers' office full of happiness and thankfulness.....like little Happy Bombs!

I'm in the full-time business of being thoughtful and appreciative so I mail out and have mailed out so many thoughtful things weekly that I literally forget that I've done it. So then the Happy Bomb goes off at the person's home or office and sometimes you hear nothing (like a dud bomb) but lots of time you get a call, text, picture, email of their happiness to have received whatever it is that was sent out. The crazy thing about these happy bombs is the timing is amazingly good. If I could remember all of the stories, I could write a book about just that, crazy great timing!

Couple stories, one happened today, I get a call from an important product line, JVC. My buddy Bob Schiendler from New Jersey runs the division at JVC that we help sell his security video cameras. He calls and tells me we have a major problem. We have a huge school district that had a bad employee (embezzled $7M) and now they want to return $100K worth of gear and, of course, they want to do this two days before Thanksgiving which is also 4 days before the end of the business month and 35 days before the end of the fiscal year. Bob, Ernie Quintana (my right hand superstar at PAR) all get on the phone. We formulate a plan and we will make something happen. We addressed the problem right away like professionals and Bob is thankful. So...What shows up literally 52 minutes later in Bob's office? It was our hand-written Thanksgiving card with a great fresh nuts and chocolate basket in the shape of Texas that was sent out five to six days earlier. So Bobs sends me a nice email thanking us and telling us the gift was unexpected, not necessary, but greatly appreciated, asking how did we know nuts were his favorite? I'm telling you that's the way happy bombs work. They literally know when the receiver needs a little "pick me up" and BAM!

We will resolve the business challenge, but crazy timing is the norm on Happy Bombs. A funny happy bomb blunder of mine was when my good friend Don Allen (successfully ran and owned a string of alarm companies and literally has never lost a nickel in business that I know of!) his son Andy Allen (a great competitor and friend) had a death in their family. Don, father and, therefore, Andy's Grand Dad passed away after a long successful life. I have always, since the early 1990s, had a ton of follow-up cards (like 100 on-hand, always) for every imaginable scenario, happy or bad, that needed to be addressed or followed up on. I mailed Don and Andy each a sympathy card, but they are father and son so I wanted the cards to be different. I grabbed two different from my stash, wrote a kind message and mailed them off. Never thought twice about it. A few weeks later Andy comes up to me at a trade show and said I got to tell you both my dad and I greatly appreciate you thinking of us, but your card to me couldn't of showed up at a better time (think happy bomb.... I will think embarrassing bomb). Andy says, "The family was gathered at my house and we were all a little down and I opened the card you sent me with the kind words, then the whole family busted out laughing when we realized you sent a, sorry for the loss of your pet card. Old Grand Dad could be a bit of a dog in his younger years!"

How embarrassing but they knew me and knew that I would have a card for that too, just got mixed up! But just like most Happy Bombs they tend to show up just when someone needs a pick me up! Happy Bombs can be anything from, birthday cards, anniversary card, thank you cards, thoughtful gifts, or my favorite... funny or joking gifts. It's such a great feeling knowing that almost multiple times a day something is arriving at someone's place that we put into motion to benefit them. The energy you receive from happy bombs is truly a gift for the launcher as much as the receiver.

25

Ozzy "When to Say 'We versus I"

Ben and I at ADI Dallas cookout event 1992. Ben is the king of WE!

There is a famous song from Ozzy Osborne called Crazy Train and it starts out: "I, I, I...." There are many people who are "Ozzies" that everything is "I did this" or "I did that".

We use we at our businesses. My boss, Ben Cornett at a company, called Intellisense (Ben, my mentor and hero, was at BGE, Intellisense, and president of Honeywell Security Division and a number of successful endeavors before and after). Ben uses the word WE. He explained to me that the word "we" is very inclusive, that it brings people together. It shares successes; it makes people feel more involved in successes and accomplishments. Winners use the word we. Losers use the word I. Funny thing the exact opposite happens when a problem arises. The same person that was all about "I, I, I" starts blaming "them, them, them" when something doesn't turn out right.

Ben Cornett, like most great coaches and successful people, flips the script. Ben would take that "we did this" and replace it with "we might of talked about it, but then I made a bad choice". Ben would always shoulder the negative or blame for the team because that's what "WE" people do. They turn into "I-people" when there is failure or blame. People will always follow, support and get behind someone who has the rare quality of giving and sharing success with others while almost exclusively taking the blame when things don't work out as planned. Look around. The world is full of good time Ozzys, the rare gem is finding WE-people that turn into Ozzys when the poop hits the fan! I challenge young people to be "We" people. The sooner you realize this phenomenon, the quicker you will ascend in whatever you are doing. You will also note that people will follow your lead and you will earn their respect. It's kind of crazy you trying to be the boastful "I" person and you get nowhere. But if you can truly change and be a "we" person you get everywhere. A great visual is the successful coach who acts like Ben, taking the blame for a team loss versus the selfish about-to-be-traded wide receiver who is the "I" guy demanding the ball.

26

Thanksgiving vs. Christmas

Pick a holiday and own it! 4th of July is a great one!

Garrett circa 2014

We always send out Thanksgiving gifts to our customers instead of Christmas gifts. Two reasons, one is that I have always been a grateful and thankful person, so Thanksgiving is probably my favorite holiday and always a great time to reflect on the folks in your life that have enhanced and made it better! Secondly, from a standing out from the crowd point it really makes sense to give business gifts at a time when the receiver isn't getting anything from anybody. Finally, a lesson I learned along the way to 50 was always to give food and try to give a good large quantity.

When you give food to an office full of people, it does one of two things. It literally gets walked around the building, allowing folks to grab a handful of whatever it is, or it gets put in the kitchen area and everyone asks, "Who sent us treats?" Then folks that might not have known of us or our company now know and positively think of us. In the beginning of the book I mentioned that it's important to do things differently than the norm and this is one of my favorite examples of that!

This past Thanksgiving we shipped out over 50 nuts baskets from The Vending Nut in Fort Worth, Texas, (www.vendingnutco.com), all with personalized handwriting thank you notes. The crazy thing this year was I got married three days before Thanksgiving. I was extremely busy, but it goes to show you that you always have time to be thankful. Thanksgiving, not Christmas.

27

No Sales No problem!

Cabo San Lucas with my family in 2015. Just like this view, this chapter is how you look at things.

Be happy they aren't using your product. I was a young guy selling glass break detectors that attach to alarm systems and my boss Ben Cornett was traveling with me in my territory in Chicago. Back then I was happy when someone was buying my product and almost felt prideful that they were. Ben asked a question (by the way that's how he would teach, by asking questions, not telling you something). How much commission did you make last month? I said whatever the amount was. He said if all we call on is people that are currently buying our product what do you think your commission check will look like next month?

Being a smart 22-year-old inexperienced sales person, I fell into his verbal trap and said "about the same". Ben went on to say with all the goals you have in life, "do you think you will be able to achieve those by being excited to see someone buying your product or more excited if they aren't buying our product?" Since that gem of a lesson, I love it when customers aren't buying my gear! This is a huge difference in the way you see things. I was so extremely fortunate to learn this lesson at age 22! When a customer says sheepishly that they aren't using my product I 100% time say enthusiastically "that's GREAT!" Let me show you where I can get you better performance and maybe save you money and launch into the features and benefits of my products.

Recently, I had a boss for one of my video camera lines that would walk into a distribution center and if he didn't see his/our product in stock, he would storm out in a huff. Literally walk out without saying goodbye. This is a 55-year-old salesman (if you want to call him that). I think that's insane. You have to earn your growth in sales every day. Very much like a house is built brick by brick, sales are built the same way.

My negative boss should have been excited when he walked into the distributor and saw a half-built house. He should have asked what he could have done to add more bricks. He should have asked if the competition was out-performing him, what could he do better or different? He should have thanked them for their information and tried to get an order for more products and taken whatever suggestion and try to implement them. Then, follow-up with a heartfelt thank-you note.

Sales, like life is a marathon, not a sprint and you have to be willing to look at things for the long haul and build your business brick by brick. In case you were wondering, mister negative boss started alienating people at a record pace and got fired. He's kicking around from company to company and will never be a successful salesperson with his outlook on life, never!

28

Don't Say No for Your Customer

My step-daughter Haylee giving a donkey a chance.

This is very much a sales situation, but can be used in many situations in life. The thought here is don't say no for someone that you want to buy something from you. Don't put up obstacles for the person that could say yes. One way of looking at this is this example. You are a young guy who wants to ask out Haylee. You wrongly (or rightly but you don't know yet) think Haylee would never go out with you, so why even ask? Don't say no for Haylee! She might say yes, so you win, or she may say no and you win, too, because you are getting experience in asking out the type of girl you are looking to date! In sales, the example is my customer who will never buy what I am selling so why ask. Being happy and successful (and yes, I believe those two things go together) is challenging enough that you shouldn't be your own biggest obstacle. I read one author call it "stinking thinking."

A recent example of saying no for your client was with my lovely wife, Crystal. She was going to get an opportunity to list a family's home for sale. Her meeting took place 10 days before Thanksgiving, so she started assuming that the clients wouldn't want to list until after the holidays. I stopped her in her tracks and said why would you want to delay the opportunity for both you and them to sell their home? She said that she just thought (insert saying no for them) they wouldn't want to be bothered over the holidays. I further asked why you think that? She said because she wouldn't want to do that. I nicely asked, "Are you selling your home or trying to sell theirs?"

I further (gently) asked if given a choice, would you rather have this whole sales process take a long time or potentially a short time. She gave me that "stop selling me look" and, said well, of course, a short time. I then said, "Stop saying no for someone that might want to say YES!" I looked at it from a lifelong optimistic salesman point of view. First close right away, sign the listing immediately (time is your enemy when you are in a competitive sales situation and you are winning, so close the deal!)

She was winning, but there were five other Realtors jockeying for this $600K house listing which pays between $9K-$18K commissions. Secondly, people have more down time to look at a house during the holidays. Hey, we all know that late spring and summer has more activity (and more competition, more houses on the market) but that time was six months away so let's make this time the best time! When you are showing your home, the home owners normally leave the home, what better time to leave their home than the holiday season. It is prime time to shop and see all the great movies that are released each and every holiday season. People tend to buy large gifts during the holiday season, right? So doesn't a house qualify as a large gift? I might Photoshop a bow on the house in the advertisements till December 25th! There's no money in "no", so don't help yourself to go broke by adding "no's" for your clients!

29

Be Charitable

Do good while you are here. Be charitable.

Combine business goals with charitable goals if possible. If you look around consistently, the most charitable people seem to also be doing very well in both happiness and financially. It's no accident! People often say I'm the most generous/charitable person they know. I take that as a great compliment, but usually point out the more I give, the better my life gets. I would hate to be known as the wealthiest person they know, and not also be Top 5 charitable person they know. The world doesn't need another stingy rich guy. I love solving multiple challenges with an idea or purpose that benefits many causes.

The GoLogo folks came back from a Haiti mission trip. They had a goal of building a house for an elderly lady named Aludes. I pulled over, stopped driving my car, so I could focus on making the goal happen. It energized and excited me to help create this charitable goal! I quickly asked how much a house in Haiti would cost and they said it would be $6K. Like any challenge you need to know the number (and add at least 20% more, because nothing comes in on the number) and break that number into small pieces, monthly or weekly amounts to hit the big number. There is an old saying, "how do you eat a cow?" Answer is "one steak at a time". This means take that huge goal and break it down to smaller size portions so it's not overwhelming.

I was thrilled that we had a year to create the money, plenty of time to achieve the goal! They added that others in their church said they would contribute. Quite honestly I don't ever factor in the financial help of others because they might flake out, or fizzle out. I look at the number and expect to achieve it on our own and anything else that is contributed is gravy! So I started asking questions, like "what if we increase prices at GoLogo?" Then I start thinking that I don't want to run off business. Poking around with more questions, we hit on the winner!

When you order logo items there is always a set up charge. We haven't raised our set-up charge in over eight years! I ask, "Have you ever had anyone complain about our set-up charge?" The answer comes back, "rarely". That's it! We will raise set up charges by a modest $5! We extrapolated the numbers and realized that if sales were the same as last year (we will grow but wanted a safe number) that $5 extra would amount to $7,200 in one year's time!

Amazingly the math worked out exactly (God winking). So every day when I recap with them, they count up the Alude money and it's a little pep in our step each and every day! Many people are real visual, so I suggested that we make a huge banner with Aludes house on it, with each story equally $1K. This allows you to see the progress and track your success. The other great benefit is people that come into the office and ask what's that? I don't know about you, but I would much rather deal with a charitable business than a non-charitable business.

They shared our plan with their group that goes to Haiti, and they were blown away by the simplicity of the plan and how quickly we were up and running with it! I love that goals and work can be combined! A little girl at church named Delaney heard about the house and wanted to donate money. We thought Delaney should color in the first $1,000 floor and she did within two months of the inception of the Aludes Project. We are now having kids color in all floors of the poster of the house to teach them to be charitable.

A few days later they told me about a whole other project they are working on trying to fund a way to capture rain water and keep it in a storage barrels in Haiti. The project is called NIW for Nothing Is Wasted. I told them "let's figure this out!" They said, you did more than enough the previous week on Alude's house plan. I responded that was nothing! Not costing me a cent, just figured out a business opportunity. Coincidently, I just brought to market two water sensing products (God winking) Waterpuck and H20ALARM.com.

To teach Haylee and Garrett about designing products, packaging, websites, wiring money, I decided to pay them a 25 cent royalty. Well I got their attention quickly when I handed them each a $1,250 royalty check. Those quarters really added up and fast! I suggest let's do a quarter on each water sensor. Next NIW meeting they were dressed as football players (remember people are visual) and told how we were donating 25 cents out of each of water sensor. Thus, they were dressed like Tony Romo who's the "quarter-back" (get it?) of the Dallas Cowboys. They challenged their group to look for small increments like a quarter that can add up. Think eating steaks not the whole cow.

At the next meeting they presented NIW a check for $1250 for NIW and $870 for Aludes home. How exciting! The energy I got from this was stronger than 4 Red Bulls! Makes me want to get more folks using our water sensors and buying more GoLogo gear. EVERYONE wins!

Another story, Chris Wilkens, who runs our Power Supply line called Preferred Power, had his best friend come to the edge of death with the H1N1 Virus. Miracle that he recovered. Chris came to me and said he wanted to help raise some money for his buddy to help with Hospital bills. Chris and I realized the Super Bowl was coming up, so we had folks buy squares with half the money going back to Chris's buddy's family. The squares idea was so successful that Chris did two full sheets, instead of one. I bought a ton of squares. What was fun was helping Chris help his dear friend. I ended up winning a square and donated it back, but another example of everyone winning while solving a great charitable cause.

I'm blessed to have a ton of charitable stories; here's a memory that was brought up a few days ago. Chris Kunz is currently a senior at Keller High School in Keller, Texas. Chris was living Chapter 28, don't say no for someone else. I walked out of a store and Chris was standing next to my Lamborghini and asked if he could take a picture. He seemed like a nice polite kid, so I decided to live Chapter 5, Encourage the next Generation, and let him not only ride in the Lambo but drive it. This isn't the charitable part of the story. Chris and I have chatted a few times and we decided that he would read this book and give input from an 18-year-old perspective, which is perfect because this has been the frame of mind I have been writing to.

Chris and I are going through pictures in my phone of products I have created, vacations, etc. and we hit on a picture of Deion Sanders and me. Chris sees that Deion is really happy in this picture. Chris asks what's up with that. I tell him the story that its very rare that a celebrity, let alone a Hall of Fame football player, is more happy to have met you than you are to have met them. Here's the charitable part. Deion was at a sports bar auctioning off Dallas Cowboy tickets for his charity. The bidding goes up and up and at the end I am the high bidder. I give Deion the money and then give him back the tickets he just handed me and said sell them again and raise double the money. Mister rough and tough football player almost cried at this token of charity. Twitter was brand new when this moment happened and Deion wanted a picture of us to Tweet. I instantly get texts and calls from people across the country who saw Deion's tweet with our picture about what went down. You got to imagine that Deion has seen a lot in his life, so when you can be charitable enough to make someone stop in their tracks, you are on the right track in life.

30

366 Days from Now

Crystal with my great friend Michael Toney's book about
Rock and Roll. Tales from the Stage. He combined meeting
his rock heroes with a goal of writing another book.

Today versus next year. I mentioned this concept earlier, but it's so very important that it deserves its own chapter. The only difference from where you are today versus where you will be this time next year are two things: the new people you meet and the information you learn. That's it! This is such a simple and powerful statement. I think about this all the time and, thus, it has its own chapter. This is the reason I devour knowledge. I love learning about others successes and try to avoid mistakes they have made. I have read a lot of biographies and let me spoil them all for you and tell you something that is in every single one of them. Every successful person has had to overcome more challenges and failures than the average person. The reason why we know names like Ray Kroc from McDonalds, Abe Lincoln (lost an astronomical amount of elections before he became President); and Southwest Airlines' great leader Herb Kelleher is simple.

It is because they chose to fail more and overcome more than what most people are willing to do! That's it! They failed more than us, but they also overcame more than us. They had failures and chose to learn from them and improve their selves. I will take a meeting with just about anyone, because a great business opportunity or friendship could emerge from that chance encounter. On the other side of the coin you have to be decisive and not get involved in bad ideas and things that will eat your precious time.

A few years before the Shark Tank television show premiered, my friend John Heilman asked me to meet with a sharp young guy who was very passionate about an energy drink that was aimed at woman. Think 5-hour energy for females. Great, right? No because the name of the drink was a negative slur for a woman that wants to date younger men. I loved the guy's energy and drive, but like a dog with a bone I couldn't refocus him on a different name or product in a less crowded field. Finally, everything he wanted to spend money on wasn't what a real business owner would spend money on. I declined to invest the $10K he was seeking. I wished him good luck and drove away with my checkbook in hand.

A few years later I was watching Shark Tank and who was on it? The guy from a few years back. He's giving his pitch and it's as if time had stood still for two years, he was in the exact same rut with the exact same numbers and challenges. Mark Cuban literally said the exact same thing to him as I did. I bring this story up for two reasons. He wouldn't listen to a word from me, someone who has achieved success and brought products to market on a small scale, or to Mark Cuban, who has done it on a larger scale. The Sharks told him the same thing and he wouldn't listen. The second thing is the great loss. By him being hard headed, he lost at least three years of his young life on a zero idea. He has since had his truck repossessed, and is living with his parents. This is a sharp young man.

Time is your biggest asset you can't get back. Getting back to the title of this chapter, who will you be 366 days from today? You will be a net result of what you chose to learn from others, through reading and meeting people and what you spent your valuable time doing. That's it! Do nothing, learn nothing, you will be in the same spot. Don't kid yourself because it's not magic. Devour knowledge and meet people, don't be shy. If you want to meet someone, go up to them and introduce yourself. I had on my refrigerator for over 10 years a sticker that said, "You miss 100% of the shots you don't take."

Be like Chris Kunz. By him stopping to take a picture of a car, he not only got to ride in that car but he got to drive that car. He's at a pivotal moment in his life and got to read and get paid to edit this book designed for young people trying to start on their own in life. What are the odds that by stopping to take a picture, you get a playbook full of ideas to help your future happen faster? The odds are zero if you don't act and you listen to that negative voice in your head that kills your dreams. Take the chance of rejection every day to make yourself a better version of you, a year from now.

31

Don't Count on Being Thanked

All the thank you notes I received in 2012.

Sparked the Haylee conversation.

I estimate that you only get about 25% of the thank yous that you have coming your way. If you are a thank you fanatic like me who sends, says, and texts tons of thank yous, you can, on occasion, catch yourself looking for that thank you to come back your way. Don't count on it, and that's cool; it's not why you did it to begin with. You get a guy a $100K job, no thank you, no bottle of wine? You give a limo and a night on the town, a $1,000 value and not even a text of "hey, thank you"? or $500 worth of Cowboy tickets...nothing? I really don't do it for the thank you, but I'm human and at times I catch myself thinking was everyone raised with bad manners? Rise above it! Don't keep score. The universe does that for you!

I have more great opportunities that come out of the blue or a distant friend connects me up with. I fully believe all this comes my way because of all the good I throw into the universe. It's a joy to do so many nice things for so many people that you literally forget what you did and a thank you note or gift comes in the mail. Every January 1st, I bag up in a clear bag the previous year's thank you notes and store them in my closet with the other years. This past year Haylee, my stepdaughter, saw me doing this and asked what I was doing. So we randomly grabbed a few notes to read and I explain to her what I did for that person. She was fascinated that there were over 100 of them. I showed her the math. That I received a thank you note roughly every third day, all year long.

Then I walked Haylee to the closet and she saw the years of thank yous. It was a nice lesson for her to see someone living what they were preaching. I asked her if she thought we were doing better in life than most. She said," yes." I asked do you think we do more for others than most people. Again she agreed. Then finally I asked, do you think it's a coincidence? She said, "No, It looks like the two go hand in hand." I agree with Haylee.

32

Ask Questions

Ben Cornett the King of questions with me circa 2013

When I was a young guy in sales, I wanted to talk and tell about what I was selling, instead of weaving questions into interactive conversation with my prospect. I think many young sales people think it's a one way street of telling their story then maybe asking for an order. There was a study done that observed conversations and then asked each person how well they thought the conversation went. They found that the person who talked more overwhelming thought the conversation went well.

Knowing this, I started asking a ton of good question on sales calls. I wanted to talk less and HAVE THEM talk more. I did it in a way that didn't feel like an interrogation, but instead tried to find out how my products could solve their problems. Another wonderful benefit of asking questions is you learn things. If you walk out of a meeting that was dominated by you talking, the other person now has all of their knowledge and they now know a lot of what you know. What did you walk out with? You walked out with 100% of what you know and a sliver of what they know. Who gained? Act that way for a year and you will be no better off than when you started the year before. If you are there talking with someone really learn, really understand. When you don't, you are cheating on building and improving your most valuable asset; yourself! Again the old saying, "God gave you two ears and one mouth, use them in the proper ratio".

There are some basic views of questions; here comes the Algebra or Calculus of questions! This is a little tricky to understand and when I first heard it from my boss Ben Cornett back in 1989, I didn't really understand how to properly implement it. Ben would say never ask a question you don't already know the answer to. I was a young sales guy who didn't know much, and I had to figure out how to ask a question that I already knew the answer to? On top of that, I have to ask a whole sales call worth of them? Oh my god....what? Let me try to explain.

Ben is a tremendous communicator and an amazing salesman. Ben is so good that you don't even realize what he's doing. People might just think he's a nice guy (which he is!). They don't understand the level of professionalism and years of perfecting his craft that's involved in never asking a question you don't know the answer to. Here is an analogy to how great people, like Ben, sell. By asking questions, it would be like taking someone through the woods and they think together you both are discovering the path through the woods and exiting the other end all the while you think you made half the choices and I made half the decisions. Conversely, with Ben or other elite salespeople they already know exactly how to go through the woods. They know exactly how long it will take and they know where they will exit, but for the person going through the woods (or the customer) they think they are on an adventure with you. In the end, with a master salesman like Ben Cornett, the client will think they got there with you and most of the time they will think they led the way. In reality, through questions (that you already knew the answers to) you were leading them all the way.

If you could earn a doctorate in sales, the salesman that never asked a question that he didn't know the answer to would be Dr. Salesman. The great ones like Ben Cornett and Lance Dean have fine-tuned their communication through the years. They have perfected their craft so they could be called Doctors, most of them are also called multi-millionaires. In the Movie 40 Year Old Virgin, Steve Carrell's character was trying to meet girls. His buddy Cal gave him the advice to just ask questions to girls. Worked like a charm on the first girl, total disaster on the next one. I bring that up because it takes time to learn how to weave questions in a sales process.

My suggestion is to listen to some of the most successful sales people you know and keep score of how many and how often they ask questions. You will recognize the patterns and you will see that the prospect feels more involved when you are asking them questions. If you talk after the sales call you find that the professional salesman knew exactly what he was doing by asking those questions. He knew the possible answers and knew the next question. I use the word "professional" salesman because anything can be used for good or bad.

A gun can protect and save, but it can murder in the wrong hands. A skilled salesman armed with questions can do both good and evil. There a huge difference between a professional salesman and a con man, just as a policeman and a murderer. Questions should be spelled Question$, because there's definitely money in them when asked correctly!

33

Be Assertive

Kyle Seay, birth mom Donna, myself and Ernie Quintana in Philadelphia circa 2012

I was going to use the word aggressive, but that can be misinterpreted, and can be mistaken for a bull in a china shop. Ernie Quintana and Kyle Seay, who I'm lucky to work with every day, define assertiveness. Those two guys are dialed in and on top of everything. A visual would be the difference between elite quarterbacks like Peyton Manning and Tom Brady and some backup QB. With the great QB it feels different because they have it together. There is a brisk pace and confidence in how they work. If aggression is a shotgun blast assertive is an assassin bullet.

Here are two recent stories about a lack of assertiveness that will probably cost two individuals great opportunities and money. In the security business, I represent 25 product lines in a four-state region. Often times, my bosses at my product lines ask for recommendations of good Representative Companies in another part of the U.S. Just a few days ago, my boss Dennis Dop, an all-around great guy who runs sales for a great company called Videofied (www.videofied.com) based in Minnesota, asked me for a suggestion in the western part of the U.S. I gave him the name of my friend, who will remain nameless.

I explained to Mister Nameless that I teed up the opportunity for him and it was all but a done deal! He was going to get eight states to represent and probably MAKE $40K annually in commission! Most people don't make $40K a year, and this is on top of everything Mister Nameless was already doing, Mister Nameless then texted me should he call Dennis? I was shocked and really made me think twice whether I should have referred this guy? I wrote back semi-sarcastically, "Only if you want the product line." If this were me I would have dialed the guy up the second I got the lead.

Say you have the product line for 10 years and you grow it, you are talking about a $500K-$800K phone call here! Can you imagine if the greatest girl in high school puts the word out she wants you to ask her to prom and you expect HER to call you?! Ridiculous. So it made me think back to when and where I learned to be assertive and I really can't think of who or when it became part of my DNA, but I can guarantee you this: if you want to achieve your goals and dreams in a sooner rather than later manner you better incorporate this as early as you can! The second example is a great distributor called TRIED has a superstar named Steven Turkasz who runs their Austin branch. I would LOVE to hire him for that market to work for me, but it's a no-no to take your distribution partners employees. Steven, who I trust and also value his opinion, referred me to a guy he thought would fit into our company. We will call him Mister Slow. I email and call Mr. Slow and many days later I get an email back saying he's interested and that he's going out of the country and will be back in a week or two. News flash, the "I'm-out-of-the country" excuse is gone. Phones and email work virtually anywhere in the world. Mr. Slow shows back up on U.S. soil and leaves a really monotone unexcited voicemail that doesn't impress me one bit. If the guy had been out of the country shouldn't his batteries been fully recharged? Why not leave an exciting voice mail and look at our website before you call and have something relevant to use in your call back.

By the way this is for a $70K job that will pay over $100K a year within two years if the person performs. What did I do after I got the unimpressive voice mail? ZERO. That's not the type of guy I want on my team. Show up on time and excited for the opportunity or I would rather compete against you than play with you. I'm willing to bet that this individual will never make a $100K a year and he was potentially a great timely phone call away.

It's truly that close in life. Make the extra call, text, follow up and be knowledgeable about who you are calling and what you want and more importantly what you can do for them. Not what they can do for you! I'm older, but you used to sell a potential employer why you were the right person to hire. Nowadays, employees act like you should sell them on why they should work for you. I disagree, if you want a great life, be assertive!

34

Watch Out for the Vice in Advice

**Cathey Briscoe, over-achiever, top Real Estate Agent, and
friend of Crystal and myself.**

Be careful of who you take advice from. When you are in a meeting really, look for people's strengths and weakness and be careful what advice you listen to from misinformed people on certain subjects. If 98.6% of the folks aren't going to get there then you sure as hell don't want to follow them over the cliff. Another thing, just because you are a great athlete that doesn't make you a great "------". What I mean by that is, if Nolan Ryan wants to teach you how to pitch hang his every word, but if he wants to teach you how to talk at a 1,000 word a minute pace maybe find someone else.

Lately, when I'm in a meeting that I'm not an important piece of the conversation, I play a game and think about each person's biggest strength at the meeting. Like today, it was with Keith Marshall (www.proficientaudio.com) and I have to say he's the best marketer I have ever met. He is great at creating and consistently marketing his line of in-wall and in-ceiling stereo speakers. The thing I learned was that the colors of the new line of speakers we were looking at we're blatantly high-jacked from a sleeve of golf balls. He loved the color combo and said why reinvent the wheel, let's use this color scheme. Here's a great marketer, giving away a huge secret.

The cover of this book was inspired by Keith's secret and my love of Godiva chocolate pretzel. So I walk out of this meeting thinking, "don't burn too much brain horsepower on your ideas look. You have your product; now look outside your industry for a look, or feel, or colors." Totally take advice from Keith on marketing, but maybe pass on child-raising since he and his wife Karen don't have kids. The point is, see people's strengths and learn from them.

I think by now you know I have a true passion for Real Estate. I see all the time people getting and giving horrible advice with real estate. So I thought about why this may be and came up with two polar opposites. First, they made some money on real estate so now they think they are an expert or, two, they had a horrible experience and lost money and now they want to warn everyone about the evils and perils of Real Estate. But the reality is they most likely have less than five transactions in their life, so does that really make you an expert or someone that should be giving advice?

Whether you lost your ass or won big isn't the sample size way too small to be giving out sage advice? Think of it this way. If your 5-year-old tried to ride a bike exactly five times, whether he did well or fell would you really want to hear about how much he knows about bike riding or would you be better off talking to Lance Armstrong? The other inherent challenge with the real estate advice is that it could be five transactions from five different markets or five different decades. The odds of you getting advice from a similar area, similar time, and similar property with the similar circumstances as yours are next to zero. People are willing to offer up advice. The smarter thing to do is to seek out advice from knowledgeable, honest experts and stick to advice from them on what they are an expert on. Watch out for the vice in advice. Ask sharp people you know if they know someone in the field you are looking for.

Just recently I decided I wanted to buy a rather large personal residence. Sounds easy right? Aren't you mister real estate? Here's the challenge. When you own a lot of properties your credit report is incredibly long. I have bank financing on many properties, but I also have 23 active mortgages on my credit report. Most people have one, maybe two. When I brought my deal to various mortgage people, they simply didn't want the hassle of doing my loan. I can't blame them. You have Family A with a few page credit report, a house, and a car or me with 23 mortgages and a 30-page credit report.

It's human nature to take the path of least resistance and a mortgage person could probably do seven deals in the time it takes to do mine. In reality, they could make more money by not doing my loan. I called Cathey Briscoe, one of the sharpest people I have ever met in Real Estate (www.lakegranburyreality.com). I asked her, "Who's the best mortgage broker you know?" She replied. "Mike Anderson (reliancemortgage.com) loves a challenge. He's your guy!" I am currently doing both a personal residence mortgage and pulling out $1.2M of equity out of 9 houses so I can go buy more. This is a perfect example of asking for good advice or referral from someone that would know a superstar like Mike Anderson. Why is Mike so great? Three reasons. He works amazingly hard for a guy that doesn't look or act like 72 years young. Secondly, Mike is going to charge me a lot of money to do my deal, because it's a complicated deal. I am perfectly fine in paying his fee. He's worth it. Thirdly, he is an overachiever and high performers likely know other high performers. Those type of people know how to get things done because obstacles, setbacks, failures never stop high-achievers for very long. Ask for advice and referrals from successful people you admire.

35

Being the Best is Duly Noted

**Ken Griffey Jr. Signed a $100 bill for a friend while playing
blackjack in Las Vegas.**

Take notes in a meeting. I learned this as a young sales guy. More times than not I ask, "Do you mind if I take notes?" One hundred percent of the time people enthusiastically say, "Yes." I like to ask (back to never asking a question you don't know an answer to) because it's like calling your shot in a game of pool. It shows purpose and intent. I intend to really understand you. I intended to fully listen to you. I intend to follow up with the important information you are saying. You immediately start the meeting on a positive note. Maybe think of the word "Note" and break it up as "Not E." As in, "Not Everyone". Not everyone takes notes, which is great for your success. You are the exception, and the successful exceptions do really well in life. Here's why taking notes works!

A. It shows you care and are paying attention to the person that you are meeting with.

B. When you write things down, you will better remember what was said without looking at your notes.

C. Constantly, I look at who take notes in any given meeting and it's the winners—like all the time! Look at Shark Tank, all of them are successful and all of them take notes, especially the billionaire. One person doesn't and that guy couldn't think anyone else is important or as "wonderful" as him.

D. You aren't a-some-of-the-time note taker. You either are or aren't. The "No" note takers will never be at the top of the game; sometimes note takers will be at best sometimes on top of their game. All the time note takers will always be on top of their game.

E. Confidence can sometimes be confused with cockiness or arrogance. Let's say you are a high-achiever and you are confident. A great way to make yourself more humble and or relatable is by taking notes. It appears to be a subservient behavior, so folks who were on the fence might be better able to see your sincerity right away.

F. Finally, what if you actually want to go back and review and the hugely critical step FOLLOW-UP. Wouldn't it be great to have a cheat sheet to look back at? If we went back and got to take first grade through 12th grade with cheat sheets would your grades be substantially better? Notes are adult business cheat sheets!

In this lifetime when all your goals, dreams, ambitions, family, and legacy is on the line and you are offered the opportunity to use a cheat sheet, why wouldn't you? A hundred dollar bill is sometimes referred to as a "C note". I note that when I see people taking notes, they tend to be more successful than others. At this writing, I am in the middle of a brutal travel run. I have been in Dallas, Houston, San Antonio, Dallas again, and Midland, Texas, all in less than 48 hours! In all this travel and theses meetings, I was the only person taking notes. Think if I put myself through that grueling schedule and I didn't take notes to follow-up and create extra business, then why put yourself through that? You have to realize it's your time, your life, your chance to achieve, and you get a cheat sheet if you want one. See the person taking notes. Bet they have more "C notes" in their pockets!

36

Are You Just Visiting?

Haylee and Garrett visiting Luxury of Leather furniture store where we were wrapped on the window. Circa 2009

The Difference between a visitor and a Salesman is a Ben Cornett special. His words live in my head each and EVERY sales call I'm on 28 years later! Ben said it, and it's true. You are just a visitor unless you sell something on a sales call. Every time I walk out of an appointment without an order or a step closer to my goal, I think I was just a Visitor today! Visitors don't get paid and if they are accidentally getting paid they won't for long. Salesmen get paid forever! I often calculate in my head whether I made money today or cost myself money today. Do your own math, if you are a salesman making 48K a year and there are roughly 240 business days a year, then you need to sell $200 worth of commission per day. Not including your expense, benefits, employers payroll taxes, etc.

The point is, are you a drag on yourself? I can guarantee if you are negative or a push for too long you won't be working for your current employer much longer. If you are self-employed, you are heading for a major problem. Easy fix, change today and start keeping score. My guys are probably sick of hearing it, but I harp on getting an order while you are at your appointment. It has already cost time, energy, gas, opportunity etc. to get to that prospects doorstep, so if you have to discount, give something away it really doesn't matter because 100 percent of the cost has already been spent whether you walk away empty handed or with an order.

Have you ever told someone you were going to do something and even though you really meant to do it for some reason you just didn't honor that commitment? I have! So has everyone else in the world if not hourly, then daily or weekly! Now relate this back to sales. "Tim, thanks for coming by. I promise to switch to your product.". Now in play is less than 100% chance they will buy what they committed to. You do this 10 times: maybe 5 in 10 will honor their commitment maybe none in 10, I promise you never 10 in 10. If we re-enact that same scenario and ask can I take an order today and bring it back to our distributor for you? Jokingly say, "They think all I do is golf, so I have to prove I was working today." Or, "my boss is a little down on me because I was sick last week sure would make things right with him if I could bring back an order." Give him a lottery ticket, Starbucks gift card, bottle of crown royal, sweep his warehouse, go wash his car ANYTHING to get some kind of order!

The only way to guarantee that he will buy and use your product is to get an order today—that's it! Today! Everything else is a wish and a prayer and something less than 100%. So many young sales guys get excited about "they are going to buy". That's like a celebration in football on the two-yard line. You get 6 points for the end zone and 0 points in the "I'm-going-to-buy-2-yard line of sales." Ask Leon Lett of the Dallas Cowboys how many Super Bowl touchdowns he has? Zero because of a premature celebration and a never quit attitude of Don Beebe. The whole world thought Seattle would run the ball in and win Super Bowl XLIX, the equivalent of the guaranteed sale. New England is the Super Bowl XLIX champs.

Don't kid yourself or confuse yourself. An order is a touchdown; everything else is worth zero points. You might be closer; you might eventually get in the end zone. But guess what has to happen now? You have to set up and run another play (run another sales call). That takes time, energy and effort that could be used elsewhere on other touchdowns because you now have to go back and score the first touchdown that you failed to score.

It happens in all industries, but I seem to notice it more with real estate agents, they jump around from agency to agency. They literally worked for five agencies in six to seven years. One hundred percent of the time when I see that they have worked for Century 21, Keller Williams, Remax, etc., I think it's the salesperson's fault that they haven't learned their basic sales skills lessons. They want to keep hopping around because it's someone else's fault they aren't successful. All I can think is they must be lacking two things: a mirror and a reality check. It isn't the successful company's fault for your lack of success. It's YOU!

Coming up in Chapter 44, I talk about You Inc. That chapter talks about investing in you. The internet, the library, and taking a successful sales person for coffee, all can help you develop your sales skills to stop being a visitor and start to close more business and improve your life.

37

No Instant Pill for Success

Ernie Quintana and Kyle Seay. Super stars at PAR who earn their success daily!

I will always try to help anyone who asks for help in trying to be more successful. I have had a lot of help along the way. I've grown to be disappointment more times than not that people in whom you invest time, money, and energy simply won't do what it takes. I will suggest books and more times than not I will send them a book for free or give them a book when I'm done with it. I think they believe their journey upward will happen instantly. I was riding with a friend over to my good buddy Lance Dean's new $1.6 million dollar house that he paid cash for and was just gaining traction with his revolutionary new alarm control panel called 2GIG. The friend I was riding with said in all seriousness, "I want to do what Lance is doing." That's like saying I want to be like the person that just pick the right lotto numbers.

Having had a ringside seat to Lance's 25-year-long overnight success, I said to my friend, "Well it starts like this. You have to go back to being a 21-year-old poor kid, and you have to outwork everyone every day! I mean everyone, and I mean every day!" You have to be the master of the breakfast meetings because everyone does lunch meetings, but breakfast is the extra five great meetings in a business week that no one but the extraordinary salesman consistently has done them for 25 years. That's 5x52x25=6500 extra meetings. Breakfast is cheap and breakfast ends, unlike dinner appointments. Then you ram as many sales calls, lunches in a day (yes, that's lunches, not lunch, and you book an 11:00, then a 1:00 lunch with two different clients) for 25 years. On top of that you invite everyone you know to Happy Hour (back when happy hour was the norm); you invite everyone because you understand the leverage of time, like Lance.

If you meet one person for one hour you have a 1 to 1 ratio and you can maybe get wealthy but it's going to take longer. So what Lance taught anyone that would notice is you invite everyone. Let's say that night you invite 15 folks and 10 show up. Now you have 10 people for that same 1 hour of time. 10 x better ratio that day and then multiple times 25 years. Lance is the best I ever saw at putting people together! Plus, you are helping those folks network with each other. Then to carry on and be this overnight 25 years-in-the-making success, you become selfless,

130

willing to help anyone who asks. Regardless of how well Lance was doing he always was and is extremely humble. Until he bought the big house, you wouldn't know that he was a multi-millionaire 15 years earlier.

There is no instant pill. It doesn't happen quickly, not that it should or you wouldn't appreciate it if it did. People who get success real fast rarely hold onto it (think lotto winners and child actors) for the long haul. I've had a run of young people lately who have lofty goals of being wealthy at a young age, like 30 years old. I'm excited these young guys have goals, but what I've been seeing is that they don't realize how much you have to develop your skill set. You have to work hard, outwork your competition, and constantly be improving yourself. For a young person to think that it's just going to happen because they are nice and pleasant is like every college football player expecting to go to the NFL. Why should it happen for you when you are giving average effort?

Fortunately, it doesn't happen fast because there are way too many lessons to learn and you would miss the strong foundations that these lessons create and teach you. Back to the car ride over to Lance's home. I could tell my friend wanted what most people do, a quick fix or an express lane to success. It just doesn't work that way, so you need to embrace the challenge and enjoy the challenge! Ninety-eight percent of the people in the world aren't willing to do what it takes to be a millionaire! Are you?!

10 Things That Require ZERO Talent

1. Being on time
2. Work ethic
3. Effort
4. Body language
5. Energy
6. Attitude
7. Passion
8. Being coachable
9. Doing extra
10. Being prepared

38

Create Freedom

My idea of freedom in the earliest 1970s is a lot different today. At least early on I could rule out being an artist!

For the last decade, I have had a sign that reads "live free" on the way to my front door. It takes time to create your perfect environment and it doesn't happen overnight. In my case, I try extremely hard to give the people around me what they want and need so that I can have what I want and need.

The late great motivational speaker Zig Ziglar tag line was "Help enough people get what they want and you will get what you want". I live it, I believe it! Even though I couldn't even carry Zig's briefcase, I was lucky enough to sit in his chair and desk at my friend Chris Roberts's office in Coppell, Texas, after Zig passed. The Blackberry phone changed my life and now the iPad and iPhone have made it so I can run my businesses from anywhere in the world, thus freedom. But none of that technology would round out my free life without the great, talented and caring people I work with.

I have been blessed to never have worked in an office in my life. Quite frankly that environment, day in and day out would bore me and sap my creativity. Some people love having a place to go to, not me. I love sales calls. When I go to someone's office, it's my favorite thing in business. Sometimes people are surprised I don't have an office. I reply: I never had someone get up, get dressed, pay for their own gas, fight traffic and come to my place, open up their checkbook and write me a check for something that I sell. I have to go to them to sell something. I look at retail sales people and it really scares me. I look at how they have to hope and pray that someone might walk into their store so that they get a chance to try to sell them something. That is absolutely frightening to me! Having so many elements of chance and luck to determine my success or lack of it in life, no thank you!

Being an outside salesman, in my mind is the greatest opportunity for a young (or old) person to create revenue, have freedom, and control your fate. Outside sales doesn't care if you are a man or woman. It doesn't care what you look like or if you are short or tall. Outside sales is freedom! It is the freedom to work your ass off and develop a skill set that can build wealth.

Back to freedom, outside sales let you pick up a sick kid from school, catch your kid's ball games. Outside sales allow you to work when and where you want. But the thing that outside sales really discovers is: can you handle the freedom of outside sales? A lot of people can't! They abuse all the great things that outside sales give you and they don't respect, and can't see the tremendous opportunity outside sales gives you! Create your perfect environment; if you aren't happy with your situation change it!

One of the best books ever written about creating work freedom is The 4 Hour Work Week by Timothy Ferriss. In his book, Tim goes from a guy working 80 hours a week barely making real money, to a guy who automates and strips out waste in his life. He creates both a source of income and the freedom and time to enjoy it. I am right now using one of his lessons. I have to get this final edit of the book you are reading done. My phone is buzzing with messages. What Tim taught me is to focus on what you are trying to accomplish today. He encourages you, in his book, to let those messages stack up and then return all your calls after you have done the most important thing you needed to do that day.

Before his book I would have felt guilty by making someone wait two hours for a return call. After his book I realized I rarely make anyone wait, and writing this book is a monumental life experience, so give yourself a break.

Final thought, if you had a horrible dream that you were locked up in a prison and that your life was predetermined by the warden on how you live, conditions you live in, and how long you had to be there. If you had a chance to avoid that prison nightmare by investing in yourself, doing the difficult things others aren't willing to do, would you? I say dream about freedom; realize it takes time and effort and embrace challenges on the road to freedom.

39

Magic Number 5

I asked Josh Randall to write a goal of how many rentals houses he would own. He not only met his goal but blew past it!

Buy five rent houses and be set for life! Seriously, just five. This is a LONG chapter. It's long because it's super important and a very easy way to be financially set for life. You don't have to invent anything, patent anything, survive on reality TV show, and have Simon Cowell think you sing well, or pick the right lotto numbers.

All you have to do is be boring and buy 5 rent houses. Remember Chapter 34 about listening to advice from people who have done what you are looking to do. I have done this very thing many times over. When someone says this won't work, ask them how many rentals they personally have? Just buy a rent house every year or two or three until you get to 5. I will tell anyone who will listen if you are doing just OK, well in life if you simply buy five quality rent houses early enough in life, 30s or 40s, you will be set for life.

There are some basic reasons why this is almost sure fire advice. First it takes discipline to stick to this investment program, and discipline to any sound investment program is a great way to build wealth. Secondly, without you really thinking about it, this action of having five rent houses is a form of leverage and, wealth is rarely created without leverage. What I mean by leverage is typically you are putting up 10-25% down payment on the rent house you are buying and the bank is putting up the rest of the money. Thirdly, someone else is paying for your retirement; the "someone else's" are the renters who will inhabit your rent houses for the next 15-30 years.

Think about this, if your employer offered you a profit sharing plan that you put 10-25% down and then they put up all the money for the next 15-30 years, would you take that deal? I can hear you now, what about leaky toilets and times that the house isn't rented? You are 100% right. That's expensive and inconvenient, and it's the same reason 95% of people won't do this Plan. But I can tell you the rewards are totally worth the hassles.

Funny thing when someone loses tons of money on a bad business deal or a stock market crash that's a "hassle and a pain" too! At least with your five rental houses you are in control instead of something that for no reason destroys a chunk of your wealth overnight. Just this week at this writing, China adjusted its currency and delivered us the rockiest stock market in years, but guess what, my houses are just fine. The fourth reason is long-term tax benefits. If you make $10K profit this year in the stock market you pay this year's taxes on that money. In addition that stock you bought you paid dollar for dollar for the stock you bought; a bank didn't give you 75 or 90 cents of that dollar—it was 100% of your money.

With rent property you are writing off depreciation and building phantom losses (the money you paid for the leaky toilet comes back tax free when you sell). You depreciate that home over 27 and half years. If the house cost $275K, then that's $10K a year of depreciation; thus, your 1st $10K of income or profits are tax free. Fifth, if you buy five great rent houses, here's what's working in your favor, rents will go up, so you might have been break even or making a little or losing a little doesn't matter because over time those rents will go up, so you will be making positive cash flow. In addition, each and every month you owe less to the bank (you are building Equity). My favorite is appreciation!

The house you bought for $169K about eight years ago is now worth $330K (an actual example, my Burney house). Finally, you are building all this wealth virtually tax-free (pay taxes on the positive cash flow IF your rents are more than your expenses that year) and when you sell (I HATE selling) because of the before-mentioned depreciation and phantom losses you cash out a fairly low-tax burden. If you borrow against the equity, you have zero tax burden. So if you have $200K equity in the house you pocket $200K, nice little retirement and you have five, so 5 X $200K equals a cool million. Congrats, you are in the top 1.4% of Americans because you were the rare individual who was willing to put up with leaky toilets.

As you read before, I had a goal of buying a house before I turned 20 and thankfully I did. It's probably the Top 5 proudest things I have done because it set a lot of great things into motion

138

at a young age. It's neat to think I left my parents' house at 18 years and 6 months and had a house at 19 years and 10 months!

I love that this chapter is No. 39 because I'm going to write about my dear friend Josh Randall (Owner of Central Screen-Printing) who is 39. But at age 31, we had a talk about what his life might look at when he was 40 years of age. Josh's family business does all the screen printing and embroidery on the items we sell through our company GOLOGO. Josh started coming down to Texas for a break from work and because he is a die-hard Dallas Cowboys fan, we would go to a game once a year. At the time of his first visit I had just turned 40 and reached my goal of having 10 rent houses by 40. By achieving that goal of 10 houses and two other business goals I rewarded myself with a Lamborghini for my 40th birthday.

So Josh showed up in Texas and we are watching some college football up in my media room and he was so stressed out he couldn't even chill out. Josh works super hard and he has four kids and a great wife named Crissy. Josh was so wound up he couldn't relax on his vacation. We had a candid conversation, because I saw all the good in my friend Josh, but if he didn't start investing, he was just going to be a good guy who works 80 hour weeks, has a nice life and some money but no real wealth.

I said, "Josh, in nine short years you are going to be 40 regardless, so you can be 40 with rent houses or you can be 40 without. Which 40 year old Josh do you want to be?" We then jumped into the Lambo and he was driving that thing 100MPH which might have helped solidify that thought.

You have to realize I have similar conversations with anyone who wants help (not always punctuated with an exhilarating Lambo drive) and almost all the time it results in no action from the person that wanted the help. It bums me out for the person who doesn't take action but it's to be expected. People want a pill, a quick solution. Josh was the rare person who took it and ran with it.

I love that this chapter is No. 39 because Josh is now 39 years old and just texted me 45 minutes ago that he bought his 71st rental today! I don't think it was a coincidence that I was right about to start Chapter 39, I call good coincidences in my life God winking at me! Josh Randall is set for life, his wife, kids, and probably grandchildren are too! All because he took the first step buying his first rent house.

On August 11th, 2014, Garrett, our 12-year-old bought his 1st rent house. It's a three-bedroom, one-bath in Central City, Ky., for $38,000. Because he is 12, I'm holding the transaction in my corporation and will transfer everything at 18. Garrett visited all of our properties in Kentucky and wanted to buy his own rent house. He has a ten-year note at 5.5%; he put $8K from his $16K in his Scottrade account. His payments are $325, plus small taxes and modest insurance. His house rented in one day for $500 a month. He will be positive at least $100 a month and have a free and clear asset at 22 years of age. His goal then is to refinance and pull $40K from his house that should be valued at $50K by then (it appraised for $45K). That $40K will be tax-free because nothing was sold, it was refinanced. He intends to put that down on a $200K house, get two roommates and live for free—all the while having two investment properties! People give me tons of reasons why they can't or don't have rent houses. I will say this, the income I earn from work allows me to live well, but the way I have built wealth is Real Estate.

40

Before Tax Dollars vs. After Tax Dollars

Standing in front of a rent house that Garrett, my step-son, bought at 12 years old. That's right 12! Never too young to start!

If you are working as an employee, you might think it's hard to start a business. It might seem daunting to get started, but I disagree. I feel like it's the easiest time to get started because you have zero pressure because your job is hopefully covering your current bills. What I would suggest, just as I did to my good friend Ray Cherry (VP sales Dallas Security and top 5 most honorable man I know) and his son-in-law Richard earlier this week was "don't quit your day job." Start building a business on the side and maybe never quit your job or quit later but do it on your terms. Most people have a family, and most businesses can't support your pay and make a profit for a few years, so do both.

Lance Dean and I always say, "Be a Top 10 percent producer at your job, so your boss will leave you alone and you can have a business on the side. I'm not a CPA, but here's a rough illustration of the difference of before and after tax dollars. When you are an employee and you make $1,000, you get taxed and after everything taken out you might get $720 of that thousand dollars and $280 went to taxes and social security. Now you go spend that $720 on cars, gas, food, etc. When you own a business, even a side business, you make that same $1,000 you then spend $1,000 on a car note, gas, food with customers you now have a profit of $0 dollars and you pay nothing on your lack of profit. You get $1K worth of spending power versus $720.

When you were strictly an employee you were paying everything in after tax dollars. The key to having a better quality of life is spending before-tax dollars from your business. I lived this lesson starting in 1992. I invented the Cart Cooly, a drink Koozie that was tapered down on the bottom to fit into a golf cart, boat and car cup holders. All the existing foam beverage holders were too large and wouldn't fit. I ran that business while always being Top 1 or 2 salesperson at Intellisense. What I noticed was while I was making $100K plus a year from Intellisense and making a modest amount from the Cart Cooly, now with all my business write-offs from the Cart Cooly, my quality of life and lifestyle soared!

With inflation and crazy taxation, I hear so many successful friends complain that they don't understand why they make really good money, but it just doesn't seem to go as far as it used to. They feel that way because it's REAL! What has happened is buying power has gone dramatically down. When I was a kid, a candy bar was 10 cents. It's now $1.39, the same bar is 14Xs more money, and people's wages haven't increased 14Xs since 1975. I encourage you to invest a little and start a small business. I discourage you from plopping down your life savings on a business you have no expertise in. Your goal is revenue coming in so that you can use those pre-taxed dollars to enjoy a better life.

INFLATION: 88% Decline in Purchasing Power of the Dollar
(a 1950 dollar now worth 11.9 cents)

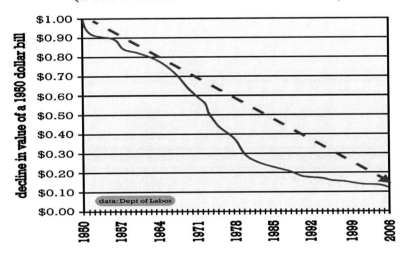

41

Find the "Why"

When I met Crystal and her two children Garrett and Haylee that became my "why"

Many times the "why" is far more important than anything else in the process. You show me someone who has achieved a high level of success for a long period of time and I guarantee you they had and have a huge "why". My first "why" in life was growing up seeing others have more than me for no other reason than the family they were born into. I wasn't mad or bitter; I was thankful I was a healthy American and knew where I started had nothing to do with me. I was happy I was in the game of life! It was just a starting point and that everything from that point on was up to me.

Some people started ahead of me some started behind, all of us had zero to do with that. If you are a young person, embrace this fact! So my early "why" was I didn't want to lead a poor financial, personal, or spiritual life. Period! I wanted to enrich myself in every aspect of my life. I wanted to enrich others along the way. With employees and people, I'm trying to build business relationships with I ask a lot of questions so I can understand their goals and dreams. I want to know what they are passionate about and see if we can align our "whys".

Ben Cornett and I joked that all success in life is figuring out what someone wants and helping them get it. We called it being a Dream Maker; if they wanted to race a car on a track, then set sales or revenue goals and reward them when they hit it. Ben, being from Louisville, Ky., made the annual first Saturday in May, the Kentucky Derby, his personal reward zone. Through the years, he took hundreds of customers and their wives. Sounds like he spent a lot of money, right? No, everything was free because the increase sales from the customers created profit that paid for it all and then some. I've made a ton of memories with special events for customers.

Just a few days prior to this writing, Chris Bartlett, a superstar salesman from Hawk Security, took his 4-year-old son Zach to his first Cowboy's game, courtesy of PAR Products. This happened as a thank you to Chris for selling a ton of our security gear. Everyone wins, except the Dallas Cowboys on that day. Think about it. If you help someone with their dreams or their why or whys you will build a tremendously loyal following. Small little example is my buddy Chris Wilkens from P3. The most important thing in his life is his family, which consists of his wife and two daughters. His WHY is his family? So Chris tells me his daughter just won a national championship in volleyball at Disney World. Wow! His "why" just had a monumental moment, so I offered to design, print, and ship championship T-shirts for him for nothing!

My why? I love helping great people with their whys. Then I asked a question? What are you all doing for the tremendous coaches who sacrificed, taught and mentored these young ladies? He mentioned a few things and I suggested having the girls autograph T-shirts and put in a shadow box and give to the coaches. Chris loved that idea. The girls get the shirts any day now and I'm as excited as they are!! I can't wait to see a group picture. Who knows what will be going on the day that pictures pops in but when it does what a great energy boost (happy bomb) that's going to be! Find your "why" and help others achieve their "why".

42

What's In It for Them?

Joe Nuccio at uptown Dallas condo.

This is a very import idea when going into almost any situation. If you are a giving-type person, you are always thinking of others. But most people aren't hard core givers so you need to focus even more on what's in it for the other person. If your child comes to you and says, "I want a new iPhone, please buy it for me." Depending on parenting (or financial situation) you may or may not consider the request. Now have that same child come to you and say I'm going to do certain chores for a month and then I'm going to come back to you and ask you to consider buying me an iPhone. It's a whole different level of chance of getting that iPhone. People always want their way or material things, but they rarely think about what's in it for the other person.

A good friend now, but I didn't know him six years ago, is Joe Nuccio. I love Joe. He's such a solid guy! He runs ASG Security, the ninth-largest alarm company in the U.S. Joe is so unassuming and honest he's a breath of fresh air. I wanted to do business with ASG. I wanted Joe to buy gear from me and I would get paid a commission. Great for me but.... What's in it for Joe? Everyone wants to sell Joe gear and get paid, stand in line! So I said to Joe, "It's great to finally meet you. I've heard nothing but great things." I stated that in the future I want to sell him more equipment, but I haven't earned that right or trust yet, so what could I do for him? What's in it for him to want to do more with me? Joe said he was looking to buy a lot of alarm companies in Texas and if I could help him with that he would both appreciate it and pay me a commission. I said thank you for the opportunity and that I would be in touch very soon. Of course, I wrote a thank you note right after our meeting. Joe just gave me the key to the front door of how to do more business with him. That occurred because of not leading with what I want out of our relationship. Instead, I chose to ask what he needed?

Like Zig Ziglar says, "You help enough people get what they want you will get what you want" I first heard Zig on an audio tape when I was a 22-year-old struggling sales person. I really had a hard time with what I was hearing coming out of my cassette player in my old white Saab 900 car. Here I was broke, not very good at my job, newly married and now I had to go help everybody else get what they wanted and then, in the end, I would get what I wanted? Are you kidding me, Zig? The more Zig talked through my stereo, the more that concept made sense. So from that day forward, I tried to always help bring value to others. I made others my priority and rewarded myself last. That formula has worked like a champ! The great byproduct of helping others all the time is people tend to really help you out because you don't come off as self-centered or the all about me guy. By always having this mental framework I feel it's been a much easier path to achieving my modest level of success. There's a great joy in helping others and in my case a lot of monetary rewards too.

Back to Joe, by resisting the urge to be selfish, I now have a very close friend. A friend for life. I sold alarm companies to ASG and got paid over $250K in commissions and sold them many more security products for many years. Just recently ASG merged into another alarm company called Protection One. I'm happy many of my friends at ASG, Bill Rose, Bob Ryan and my favorite CFO Ralph Masino had a very nice payday. I enjoyed a nice financial gain by simply asking what I could do for them first, then doing it!

43

Equity

**My friend Mike Shirley in Cancun on Pat Nolan's boat.
Circa 2013. Mike always asks for equity.**

Every job is just a job until you get equity. Always look for equity, overrides, profit sharing, high commissions or something more than just a salary or an hourly wage. Why? For one simple reason there aren't enough hours in a lifetime for most of us to get rich. Giving up all your healthy years from 16-65 for the promise of a great retirement makes zero sense to me. I made sure I'm set for life, but I want to enjoy life each and every day along the way.

My great friend Mike Shirley runs Hawk Security in the Dallas-Fort Worth area. He has run Hawk Security for over 10 years. Hawk has had three owners and none of them have given him equity. In the alarm business, you pay a monthly fee for monitoring and that is called the alarm companies re-occurring revenue. Alarm companies, when they sell, usually get between 30 and 40 times that monthly reoccurring amount.

When Mike took Hawk over it was a revolving door of managers. They had less than $10K of re-occurring revenue. Last year it sold again with $1.3M of monthly revenue at a rumored 48Xs. That's a sale price in excess of $68 million. The guy that built it had no equity; he was paid well, but when all the other people that had equity got big fat checks Mike got zero equity! What if he only had 1%? That's $680K or half of 1% $340K. You can pay off a house with half of 1 percent of the deal. I advise you to always ask for equity, override, many times management will consider it because they know you will have the company's best interest in mind because you own a piece of the company.

I took my own advice when I left Honeywell in 1997 to start my Rep Firm that I owned a 100% of. Whenever we rep a publicly traded product line, I always ask for equity in the form of stock options. I often hear no, but this year I'm 1 for 2 with "yeses." Back to Mike, it's just a matter of time before he leaves for a deal with equity. If you are that talented (and he is!) you eventually realize that you need a decent wage, overrides and, most importantly, equity! Think of it this way. If the house payments were exactly the same, which house would you like to own, the one that's worth exactly what you paid for or the home that has equity in it? Use that example with two jobs that have the same pay. Which job makes more sense? Equity or no equity? I had a friend who said the big chunks of money are the game-changers in life. Sounds obvious, but if it's obvious, why don't people focus more on setting themselves up to get theses chunks?

People tend to adjust their lifestyles up or down, based on how much they are paid monthly. But when you get a chunk from selling an investment house, equity in a business, those chunks tend to stick around and really change your life. I can almost guarantee it will be a much longer road to financial success without equity and most of the time the road will never deliver you there without equity. Focus on opportunities with equity. Create Equity opportunities as young as you can, it's a life changer!

44

YOU INC.

Never too young to starting investing in YOU INC.! My mom and a young me, 1970.

Invest in yourself; you are your number No. 1 asset. When I was a young employee, in my head I called myself Tim Shiner INC. I viewed myself as my most important asset to provide long-term happiness and wealth to myself. Nobody was interested in me being successful as much as me. I invested countless dollars on books seminars on improving my skills. Knowing every dollar spent would pay an outstanding pay off during my lifetime. Famous Author Jim Rohn says, "Learn to work harder on yourself than you do on your job. If you work hard on your job, you can make a living, but if you work hard on yourself you'll make a fortune."

In the era before cell phones when you were a traveling salesman, you had long drives and the non-investment in yourself choice was the radio. You could get really good at singing poorly someone else's song that they were getting paid every time it played. Another option was getting really pissed by listening to highly paid people bitching about politics or what went wrong with yesterday's game. If there are 32 NFL teams and one wins the Super Bowl, you are almost guaranteed to be mad about your team each and every day of your life.

The Dallas Cowboys have won the Super Bowl five times in my 50 years, so five great days out of my 18,250 days. Instead, I chose listening to sales and self-help tapes during those hours in the car. Because I am my No. 1 most-valued asset and so are you! Don't get me wrong, I love sports and I care about the country but the president doesn't care what I think and the Cowboys didn't hand me a Super Bowl ring for caring so much about their team. Team Shiner has given me a ton of happiness, experiences and wealth.

It's funny when you invest in your success and education, people think you are crazy! You paid $1,000 to go to Negotiation School? What?! They think nothing of spending $5K on season tickets for a team that has a 96% chance of not winning the Super Bowl and if they do win you aren't one ounce better for it.

When I went to Karrass Negotiation School (thanks Keith Marshall for the heads up!) I walked in with the goal that I wasn't going to pay for the class. I would pay and did pay the cool $1K, but I went in with the goal I would make that $1K back in a week with what I learned. By not thinking I have or had all the answers and being willing to always learn I went to the two-day class. I did extremely well with the lessons being taught and in less than a week I made my $1K back. I was having a sprinkler system put in a rent house and negotiated $1K off. So now that class was free and every dollar I've saved because I'm a better negotiator is mine to keep! I've saved hundreds of thousands since the class.

At this particular writing, I'm flying back from Kentucky after having bought two very nice used trailer homes from a dealership. It was a bitter cold day and negotiated the purchase of one that I wanted, then asked Tom, the owner of Austin Mobile Homes, what trailer has he had on his lot for way too long (no business man likes old inventory). He walked me to a great two-bedroom unit. The challenge for him was the unit runs on gas and many people don't like gas. I agreed that would be tough and heading to the holidays he would probably have it until spring.

What Tom didn't know was I get free gas on the site where I'm putting them (crazy Kentucky easement law, so I LOVE GAS TRAILERS). I said work me a price for the both. He did, then I said I had to sleep on it (no one else was coming in to buy those today, so don't be in a hurry). Called him the morning, worked him to split the sales tax burden and we had a deal! Collectively I saved over $4K (4x the cost of the class that was so-called expensive). Got them delivered and set up for $28K total. They will rent for $450-$550 each a month so my payback is 28 months and it's a free $1k a month for a long, long time to come.

So, why wouldn't you invest in yourself? You are responsible for your own, health, wealth and happiness. This isn't a trial run on the planet. This is it! In the test of life you should use a cheat sheet, shouldn't you?! The cheat sheet is other successful people's books, tapes, and knowledge that you can get for pennies on the dollar. Take that knowledge and invest in yourself!

45

Let them Go

**Sometimes you have to wave goodbye to bad people. Garrett
and Ronald in Uptown Dallas**

Cut loose the bad people in your life. The older you get and if you know more and more people there's a certainty that you will have people in your life who were always bad people and you didn't notice because you were too close or some people simply changed for the worst. I almost didn't write this chapter because I truly love people and want to see the best in everyone. In my 30s, I realized that I accumulated some questionable characters and was worried that some of their bad habits or simply being guilty by association was outweighing being a loyal friend.

I can't begin to tell you how hard the concept of washing your hands clean of someone was for me. I am a fiercely loyal person, but their bad choices and baggage were finally becoming my burden. I am not naming names because I hope these people can change and do right by others and society. Here are some sad stories. One lifelong buddy defrauded thousands of people in a telemarketing scheme. He went to federal prison for five years. All along I sent him money, went 600 miles to visit him, bringing rolls of quarters to buy breakfast, lunch, and dinner out of a vending machine in the prisoner visitor area. Sent him money while in prison helped him when he got out.

Our mutual friend and great friend of mine, Greg Pitto got him a crazy great job making over $100K (impossible to do right out of Federal Prison) and he proceeded to rack up over $500K worth of bad debt for the company that gave a felon a chance, while he was starting a competitive business to steal his current employer's business. All the while he was living high on the hog. Who does that to someone that gave you a chance? So this lifelong friend was in my kitchen asking for money. I gave him a few thousand bucks and said it came with a condition, you don't ever have to pay me back, but you have to get your shit together and stop hurting others or I can't be your friend anymore.

He didn't and, in fact, started a business that directly competes with my security business. His business is a non-factor, but what amazes me is how bad off are you as a person to hurt so many around you. What's the karma on these actions? It deeply upset me for a long while because I didn't understand how someone who I considered a very close friend could do so many people dirty. Just like it's important to do the right things and help people, you have to be true to your core values and beliefs and rid yourself of cancerous people in your life. It was really tough to end that friendship, but it had to be done.

Ex-friend No 2 story. In a crazy downward spiral, I had a friend that I met in the security business in San Antonio, Texas. He was a sales manager for a national security company and was heavy-handed with the people he managed, which should have been my first clue. He had bounced around to a few companies and one of the companies didn't hire him based on a personality test. It was so bad that my friend who was interviewing him pulled me aside to say it's the worst he has ever seen. He said you need to watch out. It's not if something bad going to happen, it's when. I was blown away by the stern warning. Being the loyal young friend I was at the time I looked the other way.

Once out of the security industry, he became a home builder. He built himself a huge home, drove the biggest pickup truck I've ever seen (Ford F650). There were more telltale signs along the way. He claimed he was divorced, then his wife would reappear? She was and is a sweetheart. He had an ever-present girlfriend that lived right over the border in Mexico who spoke no English, maybe that way she couldn't ask any questions. So as time went on he and I built speculation houses, first one sold and the economy turned and the next two sat forever, but eventually sold at a financial loss to me. I learned a valuable lesson about real estate. Speculation houses are a gamble, where buying quality rentals is a much more secure long-term opportunity to build wealth.

Back to my friend, he was building homes to sell between $200K and $250K. My spec houses were in the $450K area. I asked him one day, "Do you make 20 percent on the homes you build?" and he was evasive to my question. I was trying to do the math because he was doing five or six homes ($220K-$250K income) living a lifestyle like he was making millions. That should be a clue to me. Most of my true friends share the good, bad, and

158

the ugly, and we laugh at our mistakes. Well as the economy started to turn dire in 2008 people who were running shady deals started to get exposed. The first big example was Bernie Madoff, and then every shady guy after that got outed. Home builders were literally committing suicide left and right. My buddy was still flying high, until I got the phone call.

I was at my accountant Greg Thorn's office when the voice on the other side of the call said, "I need you to not ask questions and help me." My buddy asked me to pick him up in a neighborhood park on Canyon Lake, Texas, about 240 miles from my house. "Don't bring a gun (odd request) and drive me from there to a truck stop just outside the border town of Laredo, Texas. He said, "I haven't done anything wrong, but I need to flee the country tomorrow." I tried to talk my friend out of his crazy request, told him things couldn't be that bad, reminded him of all he had going for him, but to no avail.

The next day was the Friday going into the Labor Day weekend and Crystal, the kids and I went to a friend's house in Possum Kingdom Lake, Texas. The cell phone service was non-existent which created a scenario of no phones from Friday till our drive back Monday. Driving back to civilization my cell phone was blowing up! Started with they found my buddy's truck at Canyon Lake with his wallet on the dashboard. His boat was floating unmanned on the lake. Apparently all holiday weekend long there had been both search and rescue and volunteer divers looking for the body of "my friend." Concerned innocent people investigating over their holiday weekend a smoke screen of a selfish, phony person. While these good and moral people searched, my once friend was having a margarita in Mexico with his girlfriend while his wife grieved stateside."

Turns out my once friend owed everyone from honest trades people who helped him build homes, to banks, friends, family, you name it. I understand trying a business and failing. What I don't understand is living an extremely lavish lifestyle until the end and screwing everyone, instead of trying to reverse course. Scale back, be truthful and not hurt others. I was done with my business dealings with him by then, but felt for the others who weren't so lucky. His adventure ended when he flew back six to seven weeks later into San Antonio International Airport and there was a warrant waiting for him. For those of you who never have had a friend fake his own death, you will be amazed to learn it's not a crime!

The warrant was just a way to close the missing person's case, if he surfaced on US soil. My ex-friend, who chose to change his name, thought we could go back to being friends, but so many lies and bad karma was surrounding him I had to say my final goodbye. It was extremely hard to cut ties, but now that I'm older when I see glimpses of deceit, negative behavior, people challenging karma I distance myself and fast. If I look back on these two friends if I would have cut my losses after the first three crazy warning signs I would have been much better off!

I recently had a friend introduce me to an attorney. Seemed like a great fun guy. Now that I'm older and less naive I saw and heard the warning signs. He was going to rent his house and move into an apartment at 45 years old. He was playing poker three to four days a week and losing all the time, taking a lot of vacations while my other attorney buddies were working 60 hour weeks. Then I found out about the lawyer bar sanctions against him and he was three months behind on his office rent, all his employees quit. All the while he is extremely interested in doing some real estate deals with me. I immediately distance myself; he couldn't understand and I wasn't going to explain.

Later I ran into him and he again wanted to talk. I just gave him a look that said I can see through your bullshit, go to the next victim. Remember when you were young? Your parents didn't want you to hang out with the wrong people. Why? They could see what a young you couldn't. The same applies when you are older. Cut the dead wood so you have room for new healthy growth.

46

Hurry vs. No Hurry People

Two guys always in a hurry. Mike Anderson, mortgage king, and Pat Nolan, king of leverage.

Be in a hurry! Hustle! I don't know that many people who are slow and successful. I eat at the bar of restaurants more times than a table if I'm alone or it's just Crystal and me. I do it because the service is faster and better! I was recently eating dinner at a bar of an Applebee's in South Texas and the bartender was extremely slow and non-attentive to anyone, but she had plenty of time to bitch about school and how's she's having a hard time paying for it. In my mind I'm thinking stop wasting your money on school because if you can't hustle, be attentive to customers, then no matter what you are studying to be you won't be a very well-paid one of them. Higher output equals higher income.

Why do cars that go faster cost more? Because they perform! Why would society or a business pay you more? Because you perform, you bring value; you deliver faster better than the other guy or girl! Who wins the gold medal in the Olympics? It goes to the fastest person in the world. If you think college or trade school is going to deliver something special it might, but what's going to make whatever you do better is your energy level and hustle. I literally won't hire low-energy people. I have hired (and been ridiculed) people that knew nothing about our business but they had high energy and a willingness to serve others. Kyle Seay is the greatest example of that scenario at PAR Products.

Back to hustling, you only have a limited amount of time to get things done in this lifetime don't waste time! One final thought on non-hurry people, I don't know this to be true, but I think non-hurry people must make the same amount of money each day, so why be in a hurry? Commissioned sales people or business owners are probably the vast majority of Hurry people. I think the hurry people hurry because literally time is money. Be in a hurry!

47

Sell Yes or Buy No

The King of selling you on YES! Ben Cornett and me 2015 Las Vegas

You sell them on "yes" or they sell you on "no." One of my favorite things I get to do each day is recap with each the people that work in each business. The most detailed recap is the PAR one. Ernie, Kyle, Craig, Scott, and Sarah talk about what went good, great and not so well. It's a very positive call and we find ways to do things better. My old Boss Ben is always in my head on these recaps. Ben said and it's true, "In every transaction you sell them on yes or they sell you on no."

This is as true today as it was when I heard it in 1988! I listen to the guys recap their wins and temporary losses. We sold Joe some cameras, Bob said he needed to wait, so we sold Joe on Yes and Bob sold us on No. There are a lot of factors, nothing black and white, but if you aren't kidding yourself it comes back to Ben's statement in 1998. This is true if you are a 16-year-old trying to get a later curfew or a guy asking a gal to a dance, or Donald Trump trying to buy a building for less than asking price. I truly feel the sooner you recognize and realize this to be fact, the sooner you will start to master this fact of life. Buying No is the road to mediocracy. Selling yes is the road to success!

48

Get Used

My step-son Garrett, Trixie the wonder dog, and Chris Kunz, who put the book together, in front of my used 2015 Lamborghini Huracan. It had 900 miles on it when I purchased it.

Buy used cars, instead of new cars. I'm a car guy! The challenge is if you are a car guy and you buy new cars, you are either going to buy far fewer Cars in your lifetime or you will be far-less wealthy. I have bought new cars for a wife, my parents twice but never for myself once. The reason is knowledge, i.e., 95% of cars depreciate more than 33% in three years. You do that on three cars and you literally could have had a free car for NOT buying new. This works with Honda Accords, as well as Lamborghini's. For as long as I have been doing well I have had world class cars, but none of them new. Trust me. Whether it's a Porsche or Ferrari very few people really know the model year. I challenge you to look at the next 10 cars you see driving by and accurately tell which ones were bought new versus used. You can't!

That new car smell and rolling out of that dealership might be nice, but 33% depreciation-in-three-years nice? If you took the time to actually do a Financial Statement like I encouraged earlier in the book, you would realize that your car or cars aren't your friends, financially. During Thanksgiving 2013 I bought a 2003 Ferrari 360 convertible with only 3,000 miles for $95K. Today, it's worth $95K. It's been a free car! I had Acura NSXs in the mid-90s and early 2000s. The first one I lost roughly $2,500 a year or $200 a month in depreciation. The second one was FREE. I had it for five years, sold it for what I bought it for.

The reason I tell these stories isn't to brag; it's to help, I've made my fair share of mistakes in buying cars, but I've saved hundreds of thousands of dollars by buying used versus new. I bet everyone knows someone who has been "upside down" on a car—meaning you owe more than it's worth. What's worse is when that person starts rolling that negative amount into the next car. Now you feel relieved because your payments stayed the same but you went to a seven-year note from a five-year note and now you stuck $5K-$10K old debt into the new car and guess what? It's going to depreciate 30% too, but what's worse is that $5-$10K chuck is sitting in your loan like eating 64-ounce steak in your stomach at a West Texas Restaurant tourist trap!

Your friend does that a few too many times and then the day of reckoning comes. You either have to drive your current car into the ground or significantly downgrade your ride or what most people do and rob your home equity to pay down or off past car sins. The used car program works for Rolex watches too! I have had six or seven of them through the years. Always used and rarely when you sell or trade out of them do you lose 20% versus losing 50% on a new one.

I just went through security check today at the San Antonio International Airport and the agent that was patting me down said, "Nice Rolex." He didn't say, "Did you lose 50%?" or, "Did you buy it new or used?" ...just, "Nice Rolex." I'm all for having nice things, if that's what you're into; just do it financially smart so you can continue to have nice things forever!

49

Convert Pay into Assets or Income Streams

Video shoot with my wife Crystal. Creating an additional revenue stream from an automated garage door closer.

Most people work an honest day living for an honest day's pay. That is great and very honorable, but it has one huge inherited flaw. You have to go to work the next day! What if you are sick? What if you need to help a family member? What if your kids are a higher priority than work? What if.....blank?

I love working and I suspect I will work forever because I enjoy it that much, but you might not. When I was younger, I viewed getting paid as an event to go buy a nice dinner, car, home, etc. There is nothing wrong with that thinking, but it won't build wealth at all or it will take an extremely long time. I have long ago changed my thinking from how much my W2 says to how much my Personal Financial Statement states. My great friend Pat Nolan corrected me about 20 years ago. He said, "Tim, it's not what you make every year, it's how much your net worth increases and how many revenue streams you create that year that will increase net worth in the future."

I suggest you do a financial statement. When you go to a traditional bank for a business loan that will be the first thing they ask you for. It will be a sobering experience the first time you do one! You will realize that the car you have that is worth less than you owe isn't an asset. Your home that you are so proud of is really a liability more than it's an asset. It's a liability because YOU have to pay for it! Before the real estate collapse, people thought their home was an asset, but when you can't sell it for what you THINK it's worth and you have to still make the payments you realize it's a liability. I'm not saying your home can't be of value or a way to enjoy life and build equity. It can. The challenge is that you are paying for it, not someone else like a renter.

I joke that my personal home is my favorite and least favorite. It's my favorite because I love living there, but least favorite because I have to pay all of the mortgage. How do I convert my pay into income streams? My favorite, as you can tell by now, is real estate. I have covered that in the chapters before, but next would be a small business that hopefully grows up to be a big business.

Garrett, who's about to be 14, is full of inventions and ideas and why I love starting something new. I prefer to sell something existing. When the "GMAN" comes up with an invention I walk him through all the money that must be spent, e.g., patents, mold charges, websites, inventory, etc., then I go back to let's find something that costs $1 and sells for $3. I walk him through that process. You pull $1,000 out of savings, buy inventory, sell it for $3, 000, make $2,000; now buy $3,000 inventory and sell for $9,000, etc. Sounds easy, but it's not. The barrier to entry is easier than inventing something you hope not already in existence. At least this way if you fail you lose $1K instead of dumping tens or hundreds of thousands before you can possibly make your first dollars back.

This is a great example of creating an income stream—the thought of buying something for a dollar and selling it for three. It's a lot easier to find opportunity and it's easier to get started on the road to an additional revenue stream. With that income stream, you now start using that money for things you are currently paying for with after-tax dollars like cars, gas, business trips, meals, etc.

When I first started the Cart Cooly business, I was amazed at how much better my life got by making money off the koozies I was selling. It wasn't the profit that I was pocketing; it was the lifestyle I was paying for with that profit. I had a steady job selling glass break detectors that connected to security systems with Intellisense. Always Top 1 or 2 salesman (Bruce Barlow beat me on occasions. Love you Bruce!) while creating a nice revenue stream selling Cart Coolies. I believe that my performance at Intellisense was better when I had the Cart Cooly business because I had a pep in my step! I wanted to travel more because it was an opportunity to sell both Cart Coolies and glass breaks, but my day job at Intellisense paid for my trips to Austin, where my biggest Cart Cooly buyer was Golfsmith.

My life changed when I created my first active revenue stream; the Cart Cooly. I say active revenue stream because it's a business. I view investment property as passive because while you have to work at it, much less work than a side business. I just realized history repeating itself. At this writing, I have just landed in San Antonio. I am going to rent a car to drive to Del Rio to be a broker (sell an alarm company for a commission) and also tour a calendar manufacturer that will be a new supplier of an additional long-term revenue stream WWW.FREETOSCHOOL.COM. Today, I'm taking care of daily business while setting up a long-term revenue stream. This is such a natural process for me that I forget I am doing it. Just get started, start now and in time it will be natural for you, too!

Google Free personal financial statement, won't take long to fill out, but it will change your life. Garrett did his first one on his 13th birthday. He's worth $56K! We will do one on his birthday from here on out!

The Cart Cooly, invented in 1992.

50

Do It Now!

Rush final tour 2015 in Dallas with my friend Chris Wilkens, 2nd row center.

Growing up, I was a HUGE Rush fan!! There is a line in their song FREEWILL that goes like this, "If you choose not to decide, you still have made a choice".

I have embraced that line since the moment I heard it at 14 years of age. So many people think, "I won't make a decision today" or "I can get that done later." Don't kid yourself. You are consciously deciding to NOT do the thing you were thinking about. The only thing we have is time. The richest and the poorest person, the smartest, and the least smart person, the kindest, and the meanest person all have the same 24 hours in a day. The difference, in my opinion, is priorities and getting things done! Whether you're a student pushing off homework or a sales person choosing not to make another sales call, don't kid yourself. You are making an active decision NOT to do today and delaying that activity into future.

A couple of stories. My old boss, Ben, would always say, "Let's make a decision today based on what we know today. If we are wrong, we are wrong, but waiting a day, a week, and a month won't guarantee we won't be wrong then too, so why wait?" We can always fix bad decisions, but we can't fix indecision. It goes back to chapter 18 and 22 don't be afraid to make mistakes and don't daydream, DO!

I was traveling with the head person from one of my product lines. The guy I traveled with is a great salesperson, great husband, great father, and great communicator. We decided to open up more distribution for his product line that I represent. This is a big deal for both of us and quite frankly with his large family, the financial gain means more to him than me. So I'm in a hurry to get the credit applications, pricing, everything that takes weeks to process started NOW! Deals can and do cool off, so you need to minimize the down time so people don't lose their excitement.

My buddy said he would do all the paperwork when he returns to his home in two days. All the while he is in the passenger seat of my car on Facebook, commenting about a one point loss in a sporting event that his team lost to their in-state rivals the night before. That game isn't going to change and that was yesterday. Pissing and moaning about calls today isn't going to change a thing, but getting this deal done you can buy season tickets for your whole family forever. So I jumped in and emailed (while driving, I know) and got everything in motion.

It's just your mindset. It's the sense of urgency I learned to love. Before the widely famous Nike slogan "Just do it" became vogue, there was a network marketing insurance company called A.L.Williams. There spin on life insurance was take whole life insurance (build up cash value in insurance) and invest in Term (pay as you go life insurance) and invest the difference. Not to go into their program too much. I was exposed to this when I was 19 years old. Would you buy insurance from a guy, not even 20 years old?

Anyway, I chose not to do what was needed to be successful in that business, but I learned two things! First I learned compound interest and if I had started investing young (which I did), it's a lot easier to be wealthy than if I had started when I was 30 or 40. The next best thing A.L.Williams had was audio tapes. Mr. Williams was a high school football coach from Georgia before he made his millions in insurance. So his audio tapes were amazingly good! His famous line was that someone would tell him how great they were going to be at football, insurance, etc. and they would go on and on. Good ole A.L. would say, "That's great, just do it." But Mr. Williams you don't understand.... I'm going to be the best! "That's great, just do it"?

I'm not sure if the marketing people for Nike weren't spun out insurance sales people from A.L.Williams! Their world famous campaign was the second time I heard that saying. This was profound information for a motivated 19-year-old. It taught me talk is cheap, do it, and do it now! I rarely enjoy compliments because there's always room for improvement. Don't get full of yourself because there are millions of people doing it better than you!

The one compliment I do enjoy a bit is from my lifelong friend, Dave Rewers. He tells his friends that, "Tim's my buddy that actual does the things everyone else talks about." I consider that a compliment because of the time of our friendship and because it's a compliment on an activity and not an accomplishment. Activity is what you control. Accomplishment is how time judges that activity. I can only control one of those today and that's activity, and I chose to DO!

In Closing

I hope my book brought you value and a different point of view. It was a joy to relive my past and hopefully you enjoyed the stories. I believe books are to be shared, so please pass this one on to a young person with a gleam in his or her eyes. Don't be scared of your future because you can't see a clear path. Enjoy the journey! Start the journey right now!

Recommended Authors

Robert Kiyosaki, All his Rich Dad Poor Dad series

Zig Ziglar, See you at the Top

Tim Ferriss, 4 Hour Work Week

Grant Cardone, The 10X Rule

Barbara Corcoran, Shark Tales

Darren Hardy, The Compound Effect

Richard Fenton, Go For No

OG Mandino, The Greatest Salesman in the World

Tony Robbins, Unlimited Power

Dale Carnegie, How to Win Friends and Influence People

Napoleon Hill, Think and Grow Rich

Norman Vincent Peale, The Power of Positive Thinking

Cover artwork by Byron Casebier

Special Thanks to Clay Conn for enduring the reading of the first rough draft and suggesting changes. Thank you, Mark Okeefe for taking the next stab, and because he knew many of the people in this book, he really helped fine tune the book. David Sedeno and Ayesha Imtiaz also helped clean up the grammatical mistakes. Then came the Young Guns! It is extremely important to make this book relatable to young people. Chris Kunz read, gave his thoughts, and published this book online on lulu.com. At the same time, I wanted another 18-year-old Jordan Okeefe to take a crack at cleaning up the book, with his entrepreneurial zeal! Then, 16 year-old Evan Russo read and gave great input. Final read was by Jeremy Northcutt and Jim Zadeh. Thank you all for helping me achieve my goal of giving back with my book! If my book brought you more value than you paid for, and you would like to give back, any and all donations are welcome at:

Community Storehouse Food Pantry, 12073 Katy Rd. Keller, TX 76244.

817-741-0447

Donate online at:

www.communitystorehouse.org

55110301R00100

Made in the USA
San Bernardino, CA
29 October 2017